M000187267

Flogging Others

*Corporal Punishment and Cultural Identity from
Antiquity to the Present*

G. Geltner

AUP

Cover illustration: *Allegory of Virtue flogging Vice*. Attributed to Giovanni
Battista Zelotti (1526-1578) or Paolo Veronese (1528-1588). Courtesy of the Museo
Davia Bargellini, Bologna.

Cover design: Studio Jan de Boer, Amsterdam
Lay-out: Crius Group, Hulshout

Amsterdam University Press English-language titles are distributed in the US
and Canada by the University of Chicago Press.

ISBN	978 90 8964 786 3
e-ISBN	978 90 4852 594 2 (pdf)
e-ISBN	978 90 4852 595 9 (ePub)
NUR	680 | 694

© G. Geltner / Amsterdam University Press B.V., Amsterdam 2014

To all my dentists

Contents

Introduction

Corporal punishment is an evocative, almost self-explanatory term. But like other concepts with powerful and immediate connotations, it is poorly understood and rarely interrogated. Outside academia, and often within it, corporal punishment is the subject of simplistic analyses and misinformed expositions. The concept itself is ill-defined, its comparative history (as traced by historians of punishment) neglected, and there is little insight into its functions and meaning in a given cultural context, that is, beyond the exigencies of a legal or physical event. There are several explanations for this state of affairs, some obvious, others less so, as I will try to show. Yet the main threat it poses for specialist and lay audiences alike is the perpetuation of a streamlined view of punishment in general and Western penology in particular, one that tends to reflect a defensive cultural identity rather than any plausible historical trajectory. As a corrective, this brief book challenges a number of pervasive myths and lingering misconceptions about corporal punishment from a combined historical and anthropological perspective, and establishes the outlines of its complex history.

To clarify, the following pages offer an introduction to corporal punishment, mainly from a Western perspective, not a full-blown history of the measure or its applications. My goal is to trace its general contours rather than delineate the specific process by which certain societies developed or abandoned corporal penal measures. Nonetheless, the underlying historical argument of this book is that corporal punishment's path deviates greatly from the gradual decline often attributed to it during the long transition from antiquity to the present day. This may be an unsettling proposition from a Western perspective, especially regarding the period known as the Middle Ages and that straddling the Enlightenment and modernity. For despite the common perception of them being antithetical, the former by no means endorsed corporal punishment as a matter of course, while the latter's alleged birthing of the prison hardly announced the death of the rod. Indeed, far from an aberration of modernity, recourse to corporal punishment only expanded since the late eighteenth century, along with slavery, colonialism, penal incarceration, advanced science and medicine, and the nation-state. In the interim, whipping – as depicted in the Italian Renaissance image on the cover of this book – and brandishing a sword continued to be visually associated with the noblest forms of justice, thus augmenting the scepter – harking back also to a penal tool, it is often forgotten – as emblems of sovereignty, legitimate authority, and the common good.[1]

Corporal punishment persisted throughout human history also thanks to its immediate impact and low implementation costs. Yet a broader explanation for the durability of such measures emerges from the cultural-anthropological perspective espoused here, and which provides the basis for this book's second argument: Corporal punishment's resilience, even in the face of continuous criticism, can be explained by its simultaneous operation on two registers, involved as it is in two distinct processes of selfing and othering alluded to in this book's title, *Flogging Others*.[2] The first register centers on the penal act itself: The severing of limbs, branding, flogging, raping, ducking, starving, and – as we shall see – a rather diverse range of further measures, which either do not have to involve physical pain, like chemical castration, or else challenge a modern understanding of pain's source as necessarily physical, as in public shaming. In each case, the corporal penal act, which is usually part of a longer penal sequence, primarily communicates to a reference group whose norms have been violated and whose social order it ostensibly protects. It is in this sense a political act since, whatever else they do, punishment in general and corporal punishment in particular buttress claims of legitimacy and cohesiveness by indexing social others. In employing corporal punishment this way myriad societies pursue what sociologist Philip Smith describes as a broader strategy of 'shutting down liminal possibilities',[3] a process that unequivocally defines and safeguards the normative boundaries of diverse groups, from football clubs to modern nations to world religions.[4]

A second and equally important register at work is cultural. It is geared towards identifying *flogging others*, that is, those whose legal and sanctioned use of corporal punishment situates them, especially from a Western viewpoint, on the periphery of humanity and as an aberration of its process of civilization. Past and present observers of corporal punishment – and they are many, as we shall see – routinely construe such acts as symptomatic of a society, or at times of a previous ruler or regime, that undid, delayed, or undermined human progress. This ubiquitous trope of atavism reflects a need common to many societies, namely to convince themselves that their own penal measures are, on the whole, constructive and not destructive, medicinal rather than lethal, more rather than less humane. Such arguments were and apparently remain easier to sustain by juxtaposing 'our' practices with those of temporal and cultural 'others' than by positioning them in a historical or moral vacuum. The arbitrary line of legitimacy is thus subjectively drawn, with penalties differing in degree presented as diverging in kind and placed on opposite sides of an imagined normative or even civilizational divide. The primary audience of this type of saming and othering thus supposedly shares the observer's horizons, but it implicitly comprises those who do not think they are employing corporal punishment, are considering its use (or reintroduction), or are unaware of how common it actually is within their very own culture. What these groups share (or should share, according to those addressing them) is an appreciation of corporal punishment's shock value, since it is at least assumed to be occupying a place on or beyond the legitimate boundaries of their penal practices.

Both registers, the internal (social) and the external (cultural and political), have spanned different periods and regions, rendering the invocation of corporal punishment a very effective tool for forming cultural identities. By exposing the ubiquity and longevity of these registers – as this book intends to do – it is possible to spotlight the important, if hardly exclusive, role played by corporal punishment in such processes. Taken together, the negotiation of corporal punishment's meaning and its social, cultural, and political uses reveal two things. First, that there has seldom been a period, society, or polity that, figuratively and often literally, spared the rod. Secondly and perhaps paradoxically, that corporal punishment is rarely an uncontested measure, including among civilizations long perceived as hungry for or at best indifferent to pain in punishment. These two observations in turn complicate a common understanding of the pre/modern divide and challenge a prevalent view, most recently expressed by Steven Pinker, which identifies physical violence as a declining aspect of legal punishment.[5]

Why do such macro-corrections matter? There are several contexts in which current debates on corporal punishment unfold, and which tend to lack both historical insight and cultural-anthropological nuance. Among both liberal and conservative criminologists, especially in the US, a growing dissatisfaction with the prison as an effective institution for fighting crime and rehabilitating offenders has led to a reconsideration of diverse corporal-penal means, some relatively new, like non-lethal electrocution, others more traditional, namely flogging. The moral grounding as well as the short-, medium-, and long-term effects of corporal punishment are likewise at the heart of key debates among pediatricians, developmental psychologists, psychiatrists, parents, educators, and religious and community leaders concerning best practices in child rearing. To a large extent, the lines in these debates are drawn between or rather construed as separating progress from tradition, Western and non-Western cultures, modernity from premodernity, 'us' from 'them'. Advocates of various positions in such debates are thus either arguing explicitly over or making implicit assumptions about the history of corporal punishment and what kind of people and societies, past and present, employ it, be it under the aegis of official penal systems (state, church), in public and quasi-public institutions (armies, orphanages, schools), or in the private or domestic sphere. The validity of such claims is surely a matter of both intellectual honesty and broad public interest, since they inform ongoing debates, justify individual actions, and shape policy-makers' decisions and the lives of many millions around the world, including massive vulnerable populations.

There is however an equally if not more important need to reassess present-day views of corporal punishment. To a high and consistent degree, comments on the legal affliction of bodily punishments engage in branding societies that use it as culturally deficient, and by implication irrational, violent, and dangerous.[6] The most recent object of such ahistorical, narrow, and credulous treatments is the Islamicate world, as seen in the common tendency to underscore or simply accept Muslims' and Sharia law's advocacy of corporal punishment as a matter of course, a timeless given and a unique trait. A recent *New Yorker* article on Syria, for instance, epitomized the advances of a local Al Qaeda affiliate, Al Nusra, by stating that 'In Aleppo, the group has replaced failed civil institutions: its members run the police force, the power station, and a Sharia court, which has sentenced people to lashings'.[7] Surely the court's involvement in (re)creating order went beyond handing out these sentences. And yet the latter action is somehow emblematic of its recently acquired powers, both to its subjects and, perhaps especially, in Western eyes. As we shall see, however, the valorization of bodily integrity is quite explicit in Islamic thought, and there is no shortage of Muslim jurists and rulers who over the centuries have accordingly sought to reject or at least curb recourse to corporal punishment by various legal and procedural means. Their success has certainly varied; but so has that of numerous other civilizations, modern and premodern, Western and non-Western, religious and secular, which *currently* fare better in terms of their popular image in the West.

The double standard behind singling out Islamic practices today is instructive, since it owes much to the perception that other societies employing similar measures, to a greater or lesser degree, are not (or no longer, or not yet) considered threatening. In the early twenty-first-century West there is no urgent need to demonize Singapore, for instance, for its routine and legal recourse to flogging,[8] or to harp on the elaborate traditions of corporal punishment in Hinduism and Judaism, let alone among such stepping-stones to Western civilization as Ancient Greece and Rome. In 2014, it is the term 'Sharia law' that serves as code for a particularly repressive form of penal justice, and which conjures images of defaced Afghani women accused of sexual misconduct and of limbless Saudi thieves, however exceptional (and at times extra- or downright illegal) their fates might be. Small wonder that Peter Moskos, a criminologist and advocate of employing flogging *systematically* in the US penal system as an alternative to incarceration, anticipated some of his readers' concerns and preempted as follows:

> Flogging is not a slippery step toward amputation, public stoning, or sharia law. This is not the first step on a path to hell. A lesser society might go down this road by *imposing* flogging on its citizens and then descending into mob rule and blood sport. But we are a stable democracy with a longstanding tradition of deference to the rule of law. As an alternative to prison, the option of flogging does not mark a shift toward some barbaric dark age.[9]

We: A stable, modern, law-abiding, discerning democratic society. They: An infernal, sadistic, thoughtless medieval mob. Leaving aside the pandering, the facile judgments, and the hurtful language, if 'we' expand our perspective ever so slightly we will see that this kind of essentialization is widely shared among corporal punishment's modern and premodern observers, and as such has a moving target. As recently as the 1980s, Graeme Newman, likewise a criminologist and proponent of introducing electrocution as a substitute penalty into the US criminal justice system, felt no need to distance himself from an Islamic other per se. But he certainly was at pains to set apart his solution from the wanton violence and excesses of earlier periods and depict electrocution as scientific, rational, efficient, and above all equitable.[10] (In other words, like Moskos, Newman argued that it is possible to Westernize corporal punishment.) And twenty years prior to that, in a near blanket rejection of corporal punishment, English historian Christopher Hibbert claimed that, while flogging may in theory contribute to fighting recidivism, 'this is not the experience of practically every other civilized country'.[11] Britain, according to this analysis, was about to become the exception to this rule.

Debates on the present-day uses of corporal punishment in the West or from a Western perspective, then, are intrinsically tied to a broader view of history and of historical change. Yet rather than reporting truthfully about the past, many such arguments stand on a narrow historical basis and often exhibit a tendentious compulsion to draw a clear line between (and thereby group) societies that do and societies that do not employ corporal punishment. However false the dichotomy, it does underscore how much certain phenomena (including cannibalism, incest, and bestiality) have come to characterize the imagined cultural sea surrounding Western civilization. In the case of corporal punishment specifically, more than fifty years have passed since anthropologist Mary Douglas articulated the by-now canonical observation regarding ritual behavior, that '[w]hat is being carved in human flesh is an image of society'.[12] And yet, outside the circles of anthropology and religious studies, the use of flogging and branding, piercing and mutilation, shaving and painting, is immediately and at best associated with an earlier stage in what Norbert Elias famously described as the process of civilization,[13] or as aberrations of modernity. Conversely, past cultures that reputedly abolished corporal punishment are celebrated as semaphores of the Enlightenment. From an ameliorist perspective, which sees the decline of bodily punishment as both morally positive and in general a linear process corresponding to a society's degree of complexity,[14] societies that 'still' employ or that used to employ corporal punishment are easy to image as a threatening cultural, religious, or political other.

To illustrate both the ubiquity and limitations of these assumptions, let us leave the recent past and examine a popular book on corporal punishment composed in the mid-nineteenth century. *A History of the Rod in All Countries from the Earliest Periods to the Present Time* was originally published in 1840, and went through a second edition and several reprints, the latest of which appeared in 2002.[15] Its author, James Glass Bertram, writing under the pseudonym (Rev.) William M. Cooper, amassed numerous anecdotes and images of bodily penalties from world history and in different milieus and civilizations. Putting aside its limited merits as a work of history, the book displays the same ambivalence about its subject matter as can be found among late-modern promoters of corporal punishment. Accordingly, on the one hand, the licit infliction of bodily pain indicates a country's low degree of civilization; on the other, under the right circumstances corporal punishment can be used with profit by a modern, rational civilization. Cooper saw the qualitative gap underlying the distinction as grounded in the rise of nationalism and secularization. To illustrate his point, he dedicated several chapters to demonstrating how the Catholic Church, far from curbing the use of bodily pain, was in fact one of its greatest proponents: First by espousing certain ascetic practices, and later by promoting them among laymen, a gradual process that culminated in 'the Middle Ages', when 'the oft-recurring administration of corporal punishment was a portion of the every-day life',[16] at times driven by the clergy's need for sexual gratification.[17] Thankfully Humanism, the Reformation, and eventually the nation state put an end to such practices.

So much for the chronological and religious other. But Cooper is as Eurocentric as he is a modernist, and more than half the text comprises an essentializing exposition on several cultures farther afield. The Chinese, for instance, 'are governed entirely by the whip and the bamboo', a pervasiveness of pain and brutality that can only be accounted for by that people's lack of honor, a code which Europeans developed through their exposure to – medieval, as it happens, – chivalry, 'and the refined system of manners that makes it worse than death for a gentleman to receive a blow, or be convicted of telling a falsehood'. Cooper, in other words, seems to have had two Middles Ages in mind, one fomenting religious superstition and another that inspired valor and humanity, apparently without relation to Christian values. Indifference to corporal punishment, which in Europe epitomized Cooper's first version of the Middle Ages, becomes characteristic of non-Europeans generally according to his second version of the very same period. As he remarks:

> In China they have no such delicacy [associated with chivalric manners]: a blow is thought a bad thing in so far as it is painful, but no further; and in a country where there seems to be absolutely no sense of honour, there is no punishment so equal [to] and manageable [as flogging].[18]

Understandably then, Cooper considers it 'strange that the bamboo is so little used in Japan, a nation having so much resemblance to China in its manners and customs'.[19] But no matter, as Japan proves to be the exception to a fundamental rule. Readers are soon reassured that in 'India corporal punishment is one of the established institutions of the country', which explains why '[w]hipping excites no surprise [...] and hardly seems to provoke the indignation of the sufferer himself, much less of the onlooker';[20] and that '[f]lagellation in the form of the bastinade is in daily use among the Turks and Persians'.[21] Sharia law is nowhere mentioned, perhaps because this nineteenth-century observer detected more imminent dangers. Indeed, some of his strongest words are reserved for Russia: 'despotic and semi-barbaric, [it] is *par excellence* the land of the Whip and the Rod, the Russians from time immemorial having been governed by the lash.'[22]

So far the author used the rod to depict other cultures and construe them as backward and barbaric. But Cooper, like some of his late-modern successors, holds the stick at both ends, averring that it is quite possible to employ corporal punishment effectively and rationally in certain cases, or at least as a last resort, by those who are morally equipped to do so:

Although indiscriminate and injudicious flogging is bad, either in schools or in prisons, the lessons of past ages and all experience shew that a judicious administration of the Rod is calculated to further the interests of virtue and good behavior[,...for instance] in sentences for robbery with violence and similar crimes.[23]

By creating an ambiguity between differences in degree and in kind Cooper was able to argue that when violence and brutality are inherent to a culture, flogging is merely symptomatic and emblematic. Yet choosing to apply corporal punishment moderately and rationally or 'judiciously' within the context of a modern penal system is something worth considering, even if as a last resort. And lest he be charged with precipitating the Russianization of the West or leading it down a slippery path toward Chinafication, Cooper stresses the danger of flogging becoming once more 'fashionable' in Britain. After centuries of struggle to break away from the pack, it would truly be a shame to slide back into the dubious company of 'various foreign countries [where] the Rod is still the badge of power'.[24]

The transparent selectiveness of Cooper and his late-modern heirs is neither unique nor original. As we will see, employing corporal punishment as a cultural or political cudgel far predates the nineteenth, let alone the twentieth or the early twenty-first century. It is in fact a rather hackneyed technique, stretching back thousands of years and as such can be traced in a vast array of human records, from the oracle bones of Ancient China and Roman historiography, to medieval travel literature and Islamic jurisprudence, to Enlightenment-era social philosophy and modern images uploaded onto the internet. Indeed, there was scarcely a time when punishment in general and corporal punishment specifically was *not* used to other an earlier or contemporary regime or society, depicting the latter as profoundly different, brutal, and uncivilized. Thus, while corporal punishment, like many kinds of punishment, indexes social 'in's' and 'out's' within a given society, it has similarly acted throughout history as a tool for constructing selves and others, be they religious, socioeconomic, sexual, cultural, or political, lending further support – albeit only rhetorically – to the view of punishment's decreasing physicality.

Demonstrating the popularity of this mechanism across time and space is a major goal of this book. In doing so, however, I am also interested in promoting a specific corrective to the history of corporal punishment from a long-term and broad geographical perspective. In particular I wish to expose the intertwined myths of ameliorization and of premodern penal violence and repression. Regarding the former, I have already mentioned that there is a prevalent narrative of penal history as a gradual transition from repression to governance, understood in terms of abandoning actions targeting the body in favor of a rational regimen aimed at training the mind or soul. Contrary to this view, which has already been challenged by social philosopher Michel Foucault and that can be found in the writings of Émile Durkheim and Max Weber, this book marshals substantial evidence concerning the changing fortunes of corporal punishment and its supposed lack of reason. An abundance of records cast doubt on both the linearity of its decline and the presumed link between the use of corporal punishment and penal severity. As for premodern repression, there is a tendency, especially outside anthropological circles, to assume that corporal punishment is a crude form of atavism, a violent act lacking reason beyond a ruler's desire to monger fear. Among premodern societies especially, beating and flogging continually led, in the words of one observer, to mutilation, excess, and violence, in lieu of a 'clear concern with matching the numerical amount of whipping to the particular crime'.[25] Here too, diverse sources offer a fundamentally different picture, one that features not only careful regulation of such penal measures and the instruments with which to carry them out, a sustained attempt to apply it proportionately, and diverse mechanisms to opt out of it, but also a sophisticated social logic and a high degree of precision in its clandestine and public performance.

In developing these arguments, this book follows a chronological path, the better to complicate a supposed linearity in the history of corporal punishment. At the same time, it tends to work within cultures and legal traditions, which means that the unity of chronological progression is less than perfect. I begin, however, by pointing out the difficulties of defining corporal punishment, and propose to allow both history, as a provider of context, and anthropology, as a translator of social action, to be our guides. To repeat, this book is not a comprehensive history or an exhaustive anthropology of corporal punishment across time and space. Nor does it aim to explain what drove different societies at different times to reject corporal punishment or employ it instead of or alongside other penal measures. What it does offer is an exploration and illustration of attitudes towards corporal punishment cutting across the pre/modern divide, and working mostly (but not exclusively) from what is broadly accepted as a Western perspective. As such it seeks to challenge some entrenched ideas about this category of punishments and its history in present-day Western imaginations. To do so it draws on a wide range of sources, mostly textual, produced by a vast array of historical cultures. Trained as a historian of medieval Europe, my linguistic skills are limited to studying the primary sources belonging to that era and region. For most non-European cultures, I had to work with sources in translation and to rely upon a great deal of secondary literature. I tried to be discerning about the former and critical of the latter, but there are no guarantees that I have always used the best available edition or defused each and every bias shaping these texts, let alone their interpretations by modern scholars. I accept that some specialists might frown upon this, and yet hope that, despite the inevitable inaccuracies in detail, I have done these sources justice in terms of how I chose to employ them.

1. Historical and Anthropological Approaches

Problems of Definition

Corporal punishment is a misleadingly familiar term, in that it suggests a group of penal measures that is distinct from others. In practice, few punishments are not corporal. That is to say, most licit penalties – now as in the past – can involve bodily damage, brief or lasting physical alteration, or simply mild, acute, or chronic pain, even if they are not ostensibly violent or designed to be painful or generally consequential to an offender's body.[26] The slippery slope can begin from auspicious places. In the Netherlands, for instance, recent legislation obligates DUI offenders above a certain category to install so-called alcohol locks in their cars, gadgets that can determine both before and during driving what a person's blood/alcohol level is, and disable the ignition accordingly. As a control apparatus to avoid recidivism and indeed as a penal measure causing some discomfort, the alcohol key seems apt. In practice, however, the tube through which drivers must blow appears to be rather sensitive. According to one complaint, traces of cigarettes, fruit, and even ice cream may prevent the car from starting or cause it to stop, thereby imposing a much broader corporal regime than the law intended.[27]

The unintended physical consequences of the Dutch program are far from unique. Take monetary fines, by far the most common form of punishment at present (and were it to denote the full range of economic sanctions, including the confiscation or destruction of property, it would constitute the most prevalent form of punishment in human history). Fines are meant to hurt a culprit's pocket, sometimes even dramatically. But it is easy to imagine how parting with a substantial sum of money might have health implications, such as limited access to medical care (especially when health insurance is not mandatory), an imbalanced diet, or in extreme cases even hunger and disease. Depending on the particular circumstances of one's life, being fined even modestly could also require making certain lifestyle adjustments leading to increased health risks, such as how one travels, how much one works and in what kind of environment, and of course where one lives. Other dangers could be even further removed from the punishment itself but no less clear and present, for example spiraling debt and unpleasant encounters with state-, corporate-, or private collection agencies dispensing offers you cannot refuse.

Since the nineteenth century, incarceration has become the second most common punishment (after fines) in a growing number of countries around the world. Today, nearly ten million people live behind bars across the globe, more than two million (or twenty percent) of whom reside in the US alone.[28] Here too, the penal measure's possibly unintended but by now well-documented consequences include increased physical as well as mental deterioration. As regards prisons' damage to inmates' bodies we are nowhere near the level of speculation regarding the potential physical hazards of fines. Study after study and inmate testimonies, culminating in the US with the class action suit known as *Ruiz v. Estelle* (1980),[29] reveal how conditions of short-, medium-, and long-term incarceration can and often do expose inmates to extreme forms of noise and air pollution, crowdedness, physical and sexual violence, imbalanced diets, and lack of exercise. General standards of hygiene, safety, and medical care in prisons are low compared with those in society at large, and substance abuse is common. Safe sex in prison is nearly an oxymoron, as even consensual partners have limited or no access to contraception or preventative care.[30] Anyone who thinks incarceration (even without hard labor) is devoid of significant physical hardship and detrimental consequences is either completely unaware of or else in deep denial about the daily realities in many facilities. And yet imprisonment is rarely classified as a corporal punishment or discussed in such terms, especially outside specialist circles. Indeed, the bitter irony is that the prison is commonly seen as a humane substitute for the whip.

Finally, and at the risk of stating the obvious, capital punishment is itself a corporal punishment, and not merely in the semantic sense that it is 'inflicted on the body'.[31] The physical pain experienced by convicted offenders during their execution can be substantial, sometimes intentionally so. In the US, for instance, lethal injection is currently the primary method of legal execution, although its categorization as 'cruel and unusual' has been successfully defended in several courts on the grounds that the drugs used in the process cause extreme and unnecessary pain.[32] Meanwhile, firing squads, gallows, electrocutions, and gas chambers are still employed on some occasions, prefacing killing with sometimes prolonged physical, not to mention psychological, anguish.[33] Understanding capital punishment in terms of a penal sequence rather than a single event illuminates another aspect of punishment that is often overlooked in legal and analytical discussions, namely that punishment, *any* punishment, is a process rather than an act. Some legal executions are preceded by pain, and – especially in a US context – drug-induced pain only comes after many years of waiting on Death Row, under conditions whose negative physical and mental affects can be immense, as discussed in the previous paragraph. As we shall see in the next chapter, the same observation holds for other forms of punishment, which could entail financial loss and physical and psychological pain, whether or not these are stipulated in the sentence.

In other words, focusing on what appear to be staple corporal punishments – flogging, branding, dismemberment, etc. – offers a limited view of the range of physically harmful, body-altering, or simply painful practices. From a Western historical perspective, moreover, singling out corporal punishment as uniquely premodern is misleading given its prevalence in modernity on the one hand and the antiquity of other punishments associated with the modern range on the other. To begin once again with the obvious example, capital punishment can be traced to the earliest documented human civilizations, as can monetary fines and loss of privileges, for instance through banishment. But incarceration too is rather older than is commonly thought, for prisons began to proliferate in Europe as penal and coercive (as distinct from custodial and preventative) institutions in the thirteenth century at the latest.[34] The physical and non-physical pains that their regimens entailed were therefore not limited to the modern era or lost on earlier observers. Already according to the early fourth-century *Theodosian Code*, incarceration was 'a punishment [...] harsh for the innocent and too mild for the guilty',[35] and in the opinion of Gerard de Malynes, an English merchant and administrator writing in 1622, 'Imprisonment is a corporall punishment, a griefe and torture of the mind, a long and lingering dying, and sometimes a short killing by plague'. At the same time, the prison also 'overthroweth a mans reputation, and destroyeth all that is good and deare unto him'.[36] As a former inmate of London's Fleet prison, where he was incarcerated for debt, Malynes was more than likely speaking from personal experience, an experience shared by millions of inmates today.

Nonetheless, for pragmatic reasons this book is mainly concerned with the staples of corporal punishment, as seen from a modern Western perspective. The approach has the benefit of clearly profiling and then directly complicating a group of penalties that are misleadingly familiar, while avoiding an extended discussion about the presence of pain or the role of the body in punishment generally. But the choice is emphatically not meant to ignore or diminish corporal aspects in other kinds of penalties, past and present. Indeed, from the broad historical perspective this book adopts, monetary fines and incarceration are not the only penal measures whose degree of physical pain is easily overlooked. When medieval judges handed out sentences of public shaming, for instance, they knew all too well that parading a culprit before a potentially hostile crowd would likely involve significant physical discomfort (beyond inclement weather) thanks to spectators' hurling objects (as well as insults) at the processing offender. On occasion we get a glimpse of these informal protocols in action and observe how punishment looked outside law books and beyond court decisions.[37]

Finally, this book seeks to complicate the category of corporal punishment in at least one other way. Some of the available records offer a broader view of pain in punishment, one that transgresses modern notions of physical pain by underscoring the role of shame and bodily alteration as procedures that earlier cultures perceived as painful. As we survey the range of penalties that took the body rather than the psyche as their main locus (to the extent that such distinctions hold), we will see for instance, that among some Native American tribes and especially in certain medieval Islamic and Christian societies, penal shaving as well as blackening a culprit's face with ashes or charcoal was broadly perceived not merely as humiliating but as an outright form of mutilation. Distinguishing between measures that did and did not involve corporal punishment, then, requires establishing a cultural context.

Problems of Interpretation

Indeed, beyond understanding a penal act as part of a penal sequence, it is crucial to recover the unique legal, political, religious, and especially social contexts in which the act (and process) took place, and – no less important – their intended and actual social consequences. For in many ways what punishment meant depended on the perceptions and experiences of those who were involved in it, be it as culprits/subjects, state or non-state officiating agents, different stakeholders in the procedure, and its various observers, such as religious priests, the culprit's family, his or her victims and their social networks, and individuals and groups who might have economic and political interests in the prosecution of certain offenses or individuals. Unfortunately, for most of the premodern period we are rarely if ever able to recover this variety of contexts and audiences.[38] Then as now, whatever the legislator's intentions had been (retribution, deterrence, revenge, or even charity), and however unambiguous a ruler wished to render a sentence, punishments could be socially destructive or constructive, financially ruinous or mildly disruptive, politically harmful or inconsequential. Each case differed according to one's status, means, and perspective, information that we can seldom access.

From a semiotic viewpoint, however, one thing the available sources do allow us to say is that, however they came to be perceived, many forms of corporal punishment were designed, not only to hurt or alter a culprit's body, but also to employ it as a means to communicate in three discrete yet often overlapping ways. First, corporal punishment *indexes* the varieties of social otherness within a given legal culture and does so in ways that, to its intended audience at least, are far more vivid and immediate than, say, incarceration, banishment, or a monetary fine.[39] This is particularly true concerning penalties such as dismemberment and especially branding (M for a convicted murderer, T for a thief), but as we shall see it is neither limited to them nor lacks ambiguity. Either way, the premise of indexing others is that, at least to its original primary audience, the altered body comprises rather than symbolizes a penal act that is meant to eliminate ambiguities regarding that society's normative boundaries.

A second mode of communication is *mimesis* (Greek: imitation). Mimesis frequently operates in the range of bodily penalties falling under the term *lex talionis* (Latin: law of retaliation), also known as talion or the biblical principle of 'an eye for an eye' (Exodus 21:24). Punishments belonging to this category can be inflicted directly on the convict's body (a broken tooth for a broken tooth) or vicariously, that is on a conceptually related body, such as that of a spouse, a child, a brother, an accomplice, a coreligionist, or a household servant. Letting a husband whose wife was raped rape the perpetrator's wife or daughter is an extreme example of this variation, one that we will encounter later. Perched between indexing and mimesis are acts that some legal historians refer to as symbolic indexing or ironic talion. Procedures associated with this category allude to the perpetrated crime indirectly and yet unequivocally: '[S]evering the hand that strikes [...] the lip that steals a kiss [...] the pudenda of an adulterer [...] stinging by bees for stealing a hive.[40]

A third and possibly the most common principle of corporal punishment – although it is often overlooked by modern scholars commenting on premodern practices – is numerical proportionality. To be sure, it is pointless to establish a stable calculus cutting across civilizations. Thieves in our sources can be whipped or caned anywhere between five and five hundred times for ostensibly similar violations, for instance. But the broad range is only to be expected, for there is nothing universally objective or inherently more just in any of those numbers. Rather, these were conventions followed or established in a particular penal context and which reflect the relative gravity of that offense within a given tradition. That is not to say that legislators failed to develop insights, for example, about the amount of flogging a convict might be able to endure, what instruments to use, how to use them to create a modicum of equality before the rod, or how to divide beatings into sessions, the better to allow culprits to recuperate before being struck again. On numerous occasions such aspects have been clearly thought through, and evidence to that effect undermines the very common assumption that corporal punishment, especially in premodern times, lacked forethought, rationale, or proportionality.

Beyond these three modalities, punishment shed and took on meaning across diverse religious and cultural traditions and their changing approaches to the body, to relations between sin and crime, to their attitudes towards political authority, to the size of the community in question, to gender, to socioeconomic status, to domestic hierarchies, to the economic and political fortunes of the community as a whole. Few of these contexts are ever fully recoverable, let alone treatable in this brief book. Yet it is important to bear in mind that they too played a role in shaping the meaning and experience of corporal punishment beyond the trajectories of its application across time and space, trajectories, as we will now begin to observe, that scarcely follow a linear decline from antiquity to modernity.

2. Punishing Bodies

Evidence for the use of corporal punishment – flogging, branding, mutilation, dismemberment, beating, stretching, and other forms of intentional physical alteration, discomfort and pain, both brief and lasting – emerge from a very broad range of sources. These include texts, archaeological remains, and figurative art, from excavated Chinese oracle bones to digitally archived videos on the World Wide Web. The present chapter and main section of this book will trace some continuities and discontinuities attested by these diverse sources, within and across a number of cultures, regions, and religions, and with a strong focus on the Western world. It is not meant to provide anything more than a selection of case studies that test the interpretative approach related in the previous chapter and that challenges some lingering assumptions about corporal punishment's trajectory and its past and present application. Specifically, it demonstrates that corporal punishment continuously waxed and waned in different cultures at different times; and that, despite the promise of the Enlightenment and modernity, there is little evidence that we are at the tail end of a practice that has accompanied human civilization for millennia.

A key factor in corporal punishment's resilience has been its multivalence and flexibility. Corporal punishment meant different things to different cultures at different times, and it is this historical and anthropological perspective that the present chapter underscores, while demonstrating the sometimes explicit and sometimes merely implicit rationale underlying such measures. The explication is important because premodern penal acts in general and corporal punishment in particular are often seen as thoughtless and brutal, repressive rather than restorative. Yet there is much evidence illustrating, on the one hand, that there was more to such practices than atavism, and on the other that corporal penal acts, in their complexity, have boldly marched through modernity's gateway. Corporal punishment's continuous adaptability thus challenges a prevalent understanding of present-day practices of corporal punishment as a lingering and burdensome legacy of our past or at worst as a regression or an aberration in the process of civilization. A new understanding of corporal punishment that abandons a false dichotomy offers a critical viewpoint, one that will inform both penological and pedagogical debates and interrogate a salient aspect of an accepted non/Western divide.

Antiquity

It is legitimate to ask whether we can reasonably talk about ancient law codes or legal systems in ways that are comparable to the use of these terms today. The Law or a 'rule of law' may not have existed in most ancient cultures. Yet there is no doubt that earlier rulers were involved in creating and patrolling the normative boundaries of their polities just as they did their political and geographical ones, namely as part of an ongoing quest for control and legitimacy. Rulers' desire to become major power brokers in the settlement of disputes explains why ancient civilizations repeatedly produced lists of penalties or criminal legislation, since sanctions against those perceived to have violated such norms often pertained to or were at least claimed to fall under a ruler's remit. At least in this limited sense the licit or legally sanctioned affliction of bodily pain can be traced back to the very earliest civilizations whose written records have come down to us.

Chinese oracle bone inscriptions are a famous case in point. Produced under the Shang Dynasty (c. 1600-1046 BCE), these unique artefacts mention branding, severing the nose, amputating the feet, castration, and the death penalty as the era's staple punishments. Some oracle bones also bear graphic depictions of punishments, which, according to a recent study, 'reflect the cruelty with which the Shang rulers treated their people and slaves',[41] and according to another, reveal 'a sadistic orientation'.[42]

However, it was precisely such observations about the imagined cradle of their civilization that came to separate Confucian adherents and Legalists already in much earlier periods of Chinese history. The former associated the Shangs' political rise to power with brutalization, while among the latter, men such as Han Fei (281-233 BCE), argued that viewing corporal punishment as harsh was itself a sign of moral and political decline. As the Legalist adherent Li Ssu advised the founder of the Qin dynasty (221-206 BCE):

> Han –tze [i.e., Han Fei] said 'Loving mothers have prodigal sons, whereas contumacious slaves are not found in a household that maintains strict discipline' [...] According to the laws of Lord Shang persons throwing ashes on the roads were subjected to corporal punishment. Now dumping ashes is a minor crime and corporal punishment is a heavy penalty.[43]

Corporal punishment's brutality, in other words, was a matter of perspective. There were those who condoned its past uses and considered it a mild and necessary form of discipline, while others viewed it as symptomatic of a regime's (or indeed a culture's) viciousness as a way to explain its perseverance or justify its demise. Either way, the mere existence of a polemic around a ruling dynasty's penal practices illustrates first, that ancient observers were scarcely uncritical of or apathetic to flogging and maiming; and secondly, that using punishment in general and corporal punishment in particular to typify a regime's cruelty or civilizing merits was a common technique already in Ancient China.

While most Chinese regimes had no qualms about using physical torture to obtain confessions, and despite their common recourse to capital punishment, attitudes toward corporal punishment in ancient China were discerning and even ambiguous.[44] Some records suggest that, under the Han Dynasty (206 BCE-220 CE), mutilations such as tattooing and cutting off the nose and feet were thought to be cruel and were commuted to extensive beatings ('bambooing') and various forms of hard labor, measures that in theory at least do not mark a person's body permanently. The desired shift from lasting to temporary harm had unexpected consequences, however, as the abuse of bambooing could and apparently often did end with death. To address this situation, later Han ordinances repeatedly reduced the mandatory number of blows and defined the specific manner in which they were to be administered in order to ensure culprits' survival, including the precise length and width of the cane at either end and the technique the executioner must use.[45] Such strict legislation has often been interpreted as an amelioration and gradual marginalization of corporal punishment.[46] Yet it can equally be seen as a way to refine and preserve it by demonstrating a more rational, proportional, or humane approach to its execution.

All the same, there is some evidence for at least a temporary decline in the use of maiming in this period. The *T'ang-Yin-Pi-Shih*, a popular compendium of 144 legal cases stretching from *c*. 300 BCE to *c*. 1100 CE,[47] contains no instances of mutilation and only three instances of flogging, one following a son's unintentional killing of his mother in the context of an attempt to prevent her from hurting a thief (48A); a case in which a food thief is killed by his victim (48B); and in response to a youth's entry into a stranger's house at night (70A). Without offering a full survey of Chinese penal history in later periods, it would nonetheless be fair to say that throughout its changing political, social, and economic circumstances, the country's transition from antiquity to modernity never brought a real end to corporal punishment, although there were serious attempts to do so.[48] As we shall see, however, corporal punishment's perseverance is hardly limited to China, a fact that did not stop – indeed it may have encouraged – Western and Chinese publishers alike to produce images depicting its penal justice system as constantly severe.[49]

Texts produced in early Vedic India (1700-1100 BCE) exemplify how the techniques of indexing and mimesis combined in corporal punishment, with a particular emphasis on disabling

1. Chinese punishments and prisons: A view from the West.

the culprit. Standard measures included whipping, bambooing, spiking, dripping hot oil into orifices, starvation (an extremely painful form of capital punishment as well), branding, shaving, and various forms of maiming.[50] Punishments were not only broad in range but also clearly gradated according to status and recidivism, thus complicating our view of a violent, thoughtless, and disproportional regimen. A similar approach can be detected centuries later on the Subcontinent. The *Mānava-Dharmaśāstra*, an influential Buddhist law code probably dating to the second or third century CE, prescribes that, upon a culprit's failure to perform proper penance or pay the requisite fine, he is to be punished by the king as follows:

> For sex with an elder's wife, the man should be branded with the mark of a vagina; for drinking liquor, with the sign of a tavern; for stealing, with the figure of a dog's foot; and for killing a Brahmin, with the figure of a headless man.

33

The principles of gradation in punishment as well as ironic talion are once again at work. Moreover, branding in particular is meant to help enforce a more long-term measure, since, for their heinous crimes these offenders henceforth 'shall roam the earth, excluded from all activities relating to the Law'.[51] In meting out punishments of dismemberment too judges were instructed to link them either functionally or symbolically to the offending limb. For instance, someone who urinated in a forbidden place would have his penis cut off, a blasphemer would have his lips cut out, a thief his hand, and so forth. Most of these penalties, however, were never used summarily but rather had to follow proper admonition, reprove, and fines. At least in principle, only when these failed to deter or prevent recidivism could a judge resort to corporal punishment. And even then certain and telling limitations were put in place, which served to reinforce social hierarchies and boundaries. For example, the more flexible (and thus potentially more lenient) punishment of whipping was meant by default for women, infants, the mentally ill, the poor, and the sick; and hot oil and iron could only be used against (and in turn defined) major offences, such as blasphemy by a Sudra against a Brahmin or a king.[52]

Moving west, in ancient Mesopotamia, the legal prescripts of Ur-Nammu, ruler of the Sumerian city of Ur (2112-2095 BCE) and founder of its third dynasty, provide another early example of approaches to corporal punishment.[53] This casuistic ('if...then') text addresses numerous cases, running the gamut from labor to civic to criminal law, and in doing so attests the degree of judicial sophistication attendant upon a complex society. Anyone expecting a regime of physical brutality will be surprised to find very few sanctions of corporal punishment. Indeed, the vast majority of the text's eighty-five surviving promulgations prescribe monetary penalties or rewards and a mere handful order the death penalty.[54] Only three cases warranted the infliction of non-lethal physical harm:

§22. If a man fractures another man's skull in a fistfight, they will flog him 180 times;

§26. If a freedman beats a slave, they will whip him sixty times with a strap and sixty times with a belt;

§30. If a slave girl insults someone who is acting as her mistress they will rub her mouth with one *sila* of salt.

Legal texts do not always convey penal realities, but at least at the normative level it appears that Ur-Nammu's policies more often than not aimed at sparing the rod and filling the purse. Even in cases amenable to the employment of the *lex talionis*, monetary fines are often preferred. For instance, '[i]f a man breaks another man's nose with his fists, he will pay forty shekels of silver' (§19), and '[i]f a man causes the loss of another man's eye, he will pay thirty shekels' (§23). On the basis of these prescripts, it is difficult to argue that corporal punishment was an ancient ruler's path of least resistance or that those punishments that were meted out lacked proportionality or gradation.

This may not have been an isolated case in the ancient Near East. Also among the Hittites (18th-12th century BCE), flogging seems to have been an irregular punishment for theft and injury, and penal mutilation was likewise rare, to judge by extant documents and inscriptions.[55] A collection of some two hundred Hittite prescripts from the thirteenth century BCE contains but a single unambiguous reference to penal amputation, namely the practice of cutting off the nose and ears of a burglar, who, not surprisingly as we shall see, had to be a slave rather than a free person.[56] Another reference, which perhaps alludes to beating a thief with a spear (§101), describes it as a past practice, to be replaced by a monetary fine. This in turn suggests that its appearance in this context may have also served to underscore a ruler's benevolence vis-à-vis a predecessor's brutality.

Such attempts to illustrate ameliorism in punishment, or the view that identifies a general decline in brutality with advancing civilization, are a common form of self-branding already in antiquity. Understanding rulers' and cultures' representation of punishment (theirs and others') in these terms prevents potentially isolated instances from adding up to a linear view of penal history. Data about the legislation on and use of corporal punishment in this long period are scarce. But to the extent that the available sources, which are admittedly mostly normative, allow us to trace their rise and decline as a barometer for brutalization, it is hard to establish a steady course for the ancient Near East. Compared with Ur-Nammu's laws, the subsequent and more famous Laws of Hammurapi (*c.* 1780 BCE) attest greater rather than reduced support for physical brutality. Whereas corporal and even capital punishments in Ur were rarely decreed, under Hammurapi they became staple measures. However, rather than expressing a knee-jerk response to any and all violations, these prescripts for corporal punishment engaged in both indexing and mimesis, modalities that would remain influential for centuries to come.

For instance, decrees to punish a man putting another man's eye out or breaking his bones or teeth by exact retaliation (§§196, 197, 200) build on the principle behind the *lex talionis*. We can also glean a more allusive or ironic approach, such as the one characterizing the fate of the aforementioned misbehaved slave girl. Further cases of ironic talion appear in Hammurapi's text: If the son of a paramour or a prostitute disowns an adoptive parent, he would have his tongue cut out (§192); a wet-nurse concealing the death of an infant by obtaining and suckling another child will have her breasts cut off (§194); and a reckless surgeon would lose his hands (§218; and see §§193, 195, 226, 253). Last, offenders were to be maimed in body parts less immediately tied to the crime or offending limb, but in ways that nonetheless marked them as offenders of a particular stripe: A false accuser was to be branded on his brow (§127); and a slave disowning his master would have his ear cut off (§282), as would a slave striking the body of a freedman (§205). A standard calculus for flogging was uncommon in Babylonian law. Only on one occasion is it prescribed, namely when a man strikes someone of a higher social rank, in which case he was to be publicly subjected to sixty blows 'with an ox-whip' (§202).[57]

In the Middle Assyrian Period (16th-10th centuries BCE) proportionality and gradation were maintained, alongside 'a notable concern for strict equality in punishment', at least within status groups.[58] Moreover, the available records, which are both numerous and more diverse than for previous civilizations, suggest that corporal punishment was often carried out alongside non-bodily measures, such as fines, or under the guise of forced labor. Theft of movables, for instance, is punished by a combination of strokes and hard labor, and theft of less valuable items is, at least in principle, lighter, consisting of restitution, hard labor, and a few strokes. A woman convicted of hitting a man is to receive twenty blows and to be heavily fined. Besides illustrating a conventional calculus, the era provides us with examples of indexing and mimesis as well. A receiver of stolen goods would be generally defaced, and a stolen kiss would cost the culprit his own lips. A woman hurting a man's testicles would have her finger cut off, but she could also have her breasts mutilated. At times all three principles were combined, as when a malicious slanderer received forty blows, a month of hard labor, a mark of infamy on his head, and a fine of a talent of lead. As for vicarious talion, it too is attested, as when a convicted rapist had to surrender his wife to suffer what he had inflicted upon another woman.

Here as elsewhere, the gender and status of both culprit and victim played an important role in determining the penalty. Women convicted of hitting men, for instance, were liable to a double penalty: A thirty-minas fine and twenty blows with a rod.[59] Anyone hitting a free (i.e., non-slave) woman in a way that caused her to miscarry was to be punished by fifty strokes and a month's hard labor, while the same casualty befalling any married free woman could lead to the offender's wife suffering vicarious talion. Within certain limits, husbands could discipline their wives by flogging, pulling out their hair and crushing their ears; and women of the harem were allowed to discipline slaves but not to the point of killing them. Tablets preserved from the provincial town of Nuzi, in the kingdom of Arraphe (in present-day northern Iraq), establish that slaves leaving their master's home or declaring that they are not slaves could have their eyes gouged out and then (re)sold, and parents were allowed to beat

2. Severing the tongue of an offender in ancient Assyria.[61]

their children for not carrying out their duties, imprison them, send them to a workhouse, and even brand them with the mark of a slave and disinherit them.[60] In all these cases physical punishment reinscribed the ideal divisions and hierarchies of Assyrian society, reducing ambiguity – however briefly – to a minimum.

In Ancient Egypt, corporal punishment appears to have been uncommon as a form of summary justice during the Old Kingdom (2686-2181 BCE), with the possible exception of beating for tax evasion.[62] As we move forward into the Middle Kingdom, however, flogging, dismemberment, and branding become routine across what we would now call civic and criminal cases, as attested by both prescriptive and descriptive sources. A papyrus from the reign of the Pharaoh Thutmosis IV (late 14th century BCE) records the case of a soldier by the name of Mery who was subjected to one hundred blows for false litigation. Horemheb, whose reign lasted until 1292 BCE, established penalties such as mutilation of the nose and decreed that breach of contract is to be punished physically as well. Here as elsewhere, then, time brought more rather than less frequent recourse to corporal punishment.[63] To take another example, a royal decree issued under Seti I (late 13th century BCE) orders the infliction of two hundred blows, five open wounds, and a monetary fine against civil administrators who illicitly requisition free personnel or slaves, or detain a boat or its crew belonging to a foundation for Osiris of Abydos. Anyone encroaching upon the boundaries of the same foundation or stealing an animal from it was to be punished by having his or her nose and ears cut off and then being put to work as a cultivator.[64]

But are we correct in viewing this prescriptive swing in the direction of corporal punishment as one tracing a trajectory of penal escalation or brutalization? According to one specialist, earlier penalties, including denial of burial, were probably perceived by contemporaries as much harsher and more consequential than blows and amputations, since they led to 'endangering the afterlife of the deceased'.[65] The importance of this observation is not limited to complicating our view of what escalating punishment may be. For situating penal practices in a religious or cosmological context also expands the penal process's range of possible meanings. What a proper burial may be and the social and psychological significance of being denied one, for instance, could be easily overlooked by later generations or contemporaries who do not share similar views of the soul and the afterlife. Moreover, and as we shall see in later sections, religious attitudes towards the body and its integrity have continuously and profoundly influenced legal attitudes towards corporal punishment.

While legislation and application of corporal punishment in ancient China, India, Anatolia, Mesopotamia, Egypt, and elsewhere reflect various principles, no uniformity seems to emerge in terms of either practice or theory. Furthermore, no documented ancient civilization exhibits any clear linearity with regard to applying such measures. That is to say, none of them bear witness to a direct link between centralization and brutalization or between civilization and amelioration, if corporal punishment alone is to serve as an indicator. The farther we look in time and space, then, the more diverse and complex the use of corporal punishment in antiquity becomes. All the same, even this brief survey undermines the notion that punishment in general and corporal punishment specifically was little more than a display of wanton violence and fear-mongering cruelty, that it was arbitrary and disproportional, and that it reflected an absence of sophisticated cultural values.

Later Antiquity: Greece, Rome, and the Sassanian Empire

The quantity and variety of evidence surviving from Ancient and Classical Greece (8th-4th centuries BCE), Rome (8th century BCE-5th century CE), and the Sassanid Empire (3rd-7th centuries CE), illuminate new or perhaps previously hidden aspects of premodern crime and punishment.[66] Authors such as Isocrates (436-338 BCE), in his *Areopagitus* (7.39-42), and Plato (d. 347 BCE), especially in Book 9 of *The Laws*, attained a high degree of abstraction in discussing the goals of punishment and even challenged its very legitimacy as a social institution. At the legislative and practical levels, the process we can detect in this admittedly long period is not so much a reduction in usage as a sublimation and gradual disappearance of such penalties from the public sphere, accompanied by their proliferation in the private sphere, especially as applied to women, children, and non-free members of society. (In time, this process, along with Old Testament memories of ancient Egypt, provided the basis for the whip's enduring identification in the West with slavery.) The same status-based polarization characterizes Roman penal history to an even greater extent, as we shall see, and in this both Greece and Rome exhibit a trend usually associated with much later periods. Sassanian records, by contrast, allow us to talk less about status biases (though these may well have existed) in corporal punishment than about the tension between secular and religious approaches, which are strikingly different. Secular rulers were caught between their desire to portray themselves as efficient and benevolent in the exercise of punishment and the broad space given to corporal punishment in the religious scriptures by which they were also bound.

Written around the eighth century BCE, and possibly reflecting a still earlier tradition, Homer's *Iliad* and *Odyssey* portray a society heavily reliant on self-help or private vendetta, where harsh punishments were often determined and meted out quite simply by the party that could. Standard accounts of Greek legal history describe how subsequent centuries saw a gradual transition from private vendetta, to ad hoc, third-party arbitrators, to judicial assemblies, and finally to quasi-professional courts, which decided cases on the basis of increasingly detailed protocols, the most celebrated instances of which were produced under Draco in 621 BCE and Solon in 594 BCE.[67] The teleology and anachronism of such narratives has not been lost on more recent scholars.[68] Yet professionalization and centralization – even as a veneer for staunchly private affairs – seem to have been accompanied by a gradual contraction of corporal (but not capital) punishment within the public domain, that is in the case of citizens. At the same time, corporal measures became associated with summary justice carried out in the domestic sphere, especially by heads of families against offending slaves, women, and children.[69]

Over time, the growing perception of corporal punishment as a domestic affair, with its strong status bias, led free citizens, the audience of most new laws and legal procedures, to consider corporal punishment as particularly demeaning. According to Demosthenes (384-322 BCE), for instance, 'the body of a slave is made responsible for all his misdeeds, whereas corporal punishment is the last penalty to inflict on a free man' (*Speeches* 24.167; and see 8.51; 22.55). Indeed, nothing could portray a ruler in more shocking terms to elite audiences than reporting that he had flogged free men, thereby marking them as inferior and ejecting them from their status group. Here as in previous and later societies, corporal punishment engages two processes of othering, one social and aimed at indexing internal deviants, the other cultural or political and seeking to tarnish the reputation of a particular regime. Thucydides (*c*. 460-400 BCE), for example, observed how quickly one exiled soldier incited his comrades by reporting (or in this case, misreporting) that under a certain ruler '*all* were punished with stripes' (*History* 8.74.3; emphasis mine). And in the *Athenian Constitution* (35) Aristotle (384-322 BCE) ominously describes the oligarchic Thirty's rise by pointing out that they began ruling the city with three hundred 'lash-bearers' before violently crushing their opponents. Thus the relative absence of flogging in particular and corporal punishment in general from most contemporary records, including legal, dramatic, and narrative sources, is not necessarily an indication of these measures' decline.[70] Under the radar of officialdom, but with the latter's consent, corporal punishment crystallized into a highly effective mechanism for othering, a measure particularly suitable for punishing foreigners and non-free members of society, and at the same time for construing cultural and political deviants.

By and large this is a process we can detect in Ancient Rome, a civilization that consciously drew on Greek criminal law, as it did in numerous other matters. The Twelve Tables (449 BCE), a foundational text in Roman jurisprudence, prescribes beating prior to enslavement for anyone caught stealing in daylight. Slaves perpetrating the same offense are also to be scourged and then thrown off the Tarpeian Rock (II.5). Beatings are to precede execution for intentional destruction of property or grain and public verbal abuse or insult (VII.6 and 8). Last, a child shall be beaten at the discretion of the Praetor if caught destroying or appropriating another's crop at night, and then forced to pay double the cost of his action (VII.4). Yet, as a sole punishment to be meted out to free adult citizens, beating soon became taboo: As in Greece, so in Rome, accusing a ruler of causing bodily harm as a form of punishment against free men was an expedient way to taint his reign as especially, indeed extraordinarily, vicious. Here, for instance, is how Suetonius (*Caligula* 27.3-4) chose to portray the 'mad savagery' of Emperor Gaius Caligula (r. 37-41 CE) roughly a century after his demise:

After disfiguring many persons of honorable rank, by branding them in the face with hot irons, he condemned them to the mines, to work in repairing the highways, or to fight with wild beasts; or tying them by the neck and heels, in the manner of beasts carried to slaughter, he would shut them up in cages or saw them asunder. Nor were these severities merely inflicted for crimes of great enormity, but for making remarks on his public games, or for not having sworn by the genius of the emperor [...] He ordered the overseer of the spectacles and wild beasts to be scourged in fetters, during several days successively, in his own presence and did not put him to death until he was disgusted with the stench of his putrefied brain [...] A Roman knight, who had been exposed to the wild beasts, [was] crying out that he was innocent, [so Caligula] called him back, and having had his tongue cut out, remanded him to the arena.[71]

The passage contains what by now should be familiar themes and strategies. In a unique merger of othering registers, Suetonius seeks to present Caligula as inhuman: He is engaged in the animalization of free men, whom he beats, maims, and forces to behave like beasts. The shock value of such descriptions is not merely enhanced by but is entirely premised on the subjects' identity as members of the Roman elite. The extent to which Caligula and other rulers inflicted such punishments on slaves is unknown, which suggests that, at least to the elites who consumed the period's literature, such information was uninteresting.

Status continued to serve as a determining factor in the application of corporal punishment throughout Roman history. Rome's transition from Kingdom to Republic to Empire, and the immense territorial expansion accompanying this process, culminated with the formal extension of citizenship to all free men under Roman rule. Yet while the Edict of Caracalla (212 CE) broadened the political, economic, and demographic base of Rome, it also prompted a closing of the ranks among members of the elite citizenry. In the third and fourth centuries CE a distinction between a class of *honestiores* (noble) and *humiliores* (base) men restricted the latter's access to numerous legal privileges, also in the realm of penal law. In theory, flogging remained a licit penalty only as a form of summary justice reserved for punishing foreigners, slaves, and children, and various offenses by these groups would have been addressed in private by a *paterfamilias* or in public by the organ known as the *tresviri capitales*.[72] Yet there is strong evidence to suggest that *humiliores* too could be put into the latter group for penal purposes, especially with judges' new 'extraordinary' capacities. Particularly telling in this respect are some fragments left by Claudius Saturninus, a Roman jurist probably writing in the early third century CE, who authored many of the passages relevant to corporal punishment preserved in Justinian's *Digest* (6th century CE). Among his influential prescripts is one rejecting flogging as a form of summary justice above a certain rank: 'All those whom it is not permitted to punish by whipping are persons that should have the same respect shown them that decurions have'.[73] In other words, it was not or rather no longer enough to be a free citizen in order to avoid this humiliating form of punishment; the massive expansion of Roman citizenship prompted at best only a minor reduction in the use of corporal punishment, while maintaining the key function of social othering.

The political register of corporal punishment likewise remained relevant, serving as an indicator of a ruler's cruelty. According to early Church historian Eusebius of Caesarea (260/265-340), under the late pagan emperor Maximinus Daia (r. 308-313), mutilation was introduced as an alternative to capital punishment (*Historia Ecclesiastica* 8.12.10). And late Roman Christian emperors and legal codifiers Theodosius (r. 379-395) and Justinian (r. 527-565) promulgated legal prescripts that sanctioned flogging, for instance against pimps (Novel 18 and Novel 14, respectively), as a commuted sentence for culprits unable to pay their fine (*Codex* 9.19.6), and as a regular penalty (*Digest* 48.19.7 and 28.8; 48.1.2; 48.7.1). These highly influential texts also prescribed castration as a retaliatory measure as well as a penalty for an incestuous marriage (Novel 142 and 154), and dismemberment, for instance against those disseminating heresy, albeit in a way that enabled culprits to continue to support themselves (Novel 42.2, 128.20, 134.13). Under Justinian in particular it was the abuse rather than the use of such measures that came under attack. Procopius of Caesarea (d. c. 560) claimed in his *Secret History* (11.36 and 16.19-21) that Justinian and his wife Theodora employed castration and flogging as penalties for pederasty (which in itself he found acceptable) in ways that were apparently designed to taint certain political factions. Once again, we can observe corporal punishment operating in both a social and a political register.

The Sassanian Empire's extant monuments include several texts that shed further light on attitudes towards crime and punishment in Late Antiquity. Often undergirding these works is the inseparability of Zoroastrian religion and the state, entities that, according to the seventh-century *Letter of Tansar*, 'were born of the same womb, joined together and never to be sundered'.[74] Crime, accordingly, is often equated with sin, and criminals could easily be charged and prosecuted as apostates, while punishment operated as a necessary means to restore an ancient order, one preceding the moral deterioration of humanity:

> Know that the ancients refrained from this [i.e., punishment] because the people were not given to disobedience and breach of good order [...but w]hen corruption became rife and men ceased to submit to Religion, Reason and the State, and all sense of values disappeared, it was only through bloodshed that honour could be restored to such a realm [...] Punishment and bloodshed among people of this kind, even if of a prodigality that seems to have no bound, is recognized by us as life and health [...] For in days to come the foundations of State and Religion will be in every way strengthened through this; and the more the punishment he [i.e. the good ruler] inflicts to make each estate return to its own sphere, the more the praise he will receive.[75]

Paradoxically, however, in striving to restore this ancient order, the idealized Sassanian emperor, also known as the King of Kings, has produced 'a law far better than that of the ancients'.[76] Here, once again, we can observe how striving for political and religious legitimacy employs punishment to simultaneously cast a shadow on a previous regime and bolster a present one. Instead of a swift death as a matter of course for convicted heretics, for instance, the benign ruler introduced imprisonment for one year, followed by repeated attempts at conversion. The success of the latter leads to freedom, but its failure to death. As for corporal punishments, instead of a strict regime modeled on the *lex talionis*:

> He laid down a law whereby for a wound there is a fixed fine in proportion to it, so that the wrongdoer may suffer from that and the victim will receive benefit and comfort. It is not now as when they cut off a thief's hand, benefiting none and causing great loss among the people.

Proportionality, reason, and a certain degree of compassion combine to offer a new blueprint for justice. Reintegration of culprits and apostates becomes an important, if not overriding, concern, as select brigands are forgiven while others are executed, and 'no member is severed whereby capacity would be diminished. Thus they [i.e., the culprits] are ashamed and disgraced, but yet no loss befalls their work and activity', even in the case of recidivists.[77]

Similar principles are at work in *The Book of a Thousand Judgements*, a text probably compiled in the eleventh century as an attempt to capture certain practices in pre-Islamic Iran. Dismemberment is nowhere mentioned, and although branding is discussed as a licit punishment to be used, for instance, against a Zoroastrian seller and a non-Zoroastrian buyer of a slave (XVI, 1, 13-15), and judges are allowed to 'set a mark' upon convicted sorcerers (LII, A25, 16 – 26, 11), use of the measure is clearly being curbed. The text denies plaintiffs any recourse to branding against a debtor in 'minor matters' (XVIII, 3, 5-6) and states that even if a person commits the same offense for which he has already been branded four times, his punishment can only escalate to perpetual imprisonment (XLVI, 73, 1-2). For any act of physical violence, moreover, including 'the pulling out of the beard and hair', disfigurement, pain, and the spilling of blood, a monetary fine must be paid (L, A14, 15 – 15, 1). Here too, then, corporal talion largely disappears from the penal landscape, perhaps as a comment on a more contemporary regime.

One striking thing about these legal texts is how sharply (and perhaps intentionally) they contrast with prescriptions for piercing and cutting out the tongues of heretics and the ubiquitous and sometimes even fantastic use of flogging in the Zoroastrian *Avesta* tradition.[78] These works contain innumerable instances in which lashes are decreed for offenses ranging from breach of contract to assault to apostasy. For instance, the high Zoroastrian deity Ahura Mazda prescribes five lashes with two kinds of whips against anyone who acts in a threatening manner (*agerepta*). If he repeats the offense, he is to receive ten lashes by each whip, then fifteen, thirty, fifty, sixty, and ninety, respectively for each violation. For the eighth consecutive offense, unless the perpetrator had already atoned for previous ones, he is liable to two hundred lashes from each whip, and refusing to atone likewise earns the culprit two hundred lashes per whip.[79] As elsewhere in the ancient world, gradation and proportionality are guiding principles in corporal punishment, although beyond a certain number of lashes, internal logic begins to collapse before the implausibility of the proposed penal act, which could reach many hundreds and at times over one thousand blows.

Religion and Corporal Punishment

We have already had a chance to observe the importance of situating penal practices in a religious context as well. By incorporating this perspective the fuller meaning, for instance, of denying someone a proper burial in ancient Egypt comes to light; and it is only by juxtaposing religious and quasi-secular texts that the alleged scope of Sassanian reforms in penal law becomes apparent. In this book corporal punishment is treated in terms of a practice largely administered by a leader or a regime with sufficient claims to legitimate political authority. But since religious and political establishments (often distinguished in a Western context as church and state) were and remain intertwined to varying degrees, the secular meaning of punishment is hard to separate from the religious ideas shaping audiences' and participants' expectations. That is not to say that religion's influence on penal matters was constant or consistent through time and space. External political and economic circumstances as well as internal reforms and reorientations throughout history meant that both the scale and direction of influence tended to stay in flux.

Nonetheless, there are several religious dimensions to punishment that deserve attention. The first and broadest concerns the relations between crime (social deviancy) and sin (religious or theological deviancy) and the extent to which they define the ideal relationship between church and state, religious and secular authorities and establishments. To what extent, for instance, is the state perceived as a vehicle for spiritual orientation, driven by doctrinal principles on the one hand and eschatological expectations on the other? Are all criminals sinners or indeed heretics because the state is morally and politically subordinate to the church, or is the opposite true, in which case religious deviants become, *in extremis*, traitors? Or should these categories never overlap? A second and related element has to do with institutional practices of punishment. Did priests, for example, participate in secular punishment and if so how (as judges, executioners, paralegals, spectators, etc.)? And what were the relations between penal practices among the clerical rank and file (if such existed) and those who were not members of these groups? Finally, attitudes that religious traditions promote towards the body can also endow certain acts of corporal punishment or certain physical attributes with special meaning, be it positive or negative.[80] For instance, are bodies sacred and as such cannot be licitly manipulated? Or are they innately corrupt, and therefore present a major obstacle to moral and spiritual self-fulfillment? Should impairments or deformities be understood as moral indicators of human weakness or rather as signs of divine clemency and even preference?[81] The present section illuminates these aspects by briefly examining corporal punishment in Judaism, Christianity, and Islam, three religious traditions that have both shaped and absorbed Western penal practices.

Judaism

The early pages of the Pentateuch describe what is perhaps the most famous act of branding in the Western tradition, namely the marking of Cain. It is, however, a rather ambiguous incident from a penal perspective. After slaying his brother Abel, Cain is sentenced by God to be a 'restless wanderer on earth' (Genesis 4:12). Cain objects that the punishment is too onerous since being out of God's sight (which was apparently limited) meant certain death, though at the hands of whom, exactly, is not clear, given that the world's human population at that time consisted of Cain's parents and perhaps a younger sibling. God, at any rate, was convinced by the argument and, without altering the literal sentence, declared that any harm caused to Cain would be avenged sevenfold. He furthermore put an unspecified mark on Cain explicitly so 'that whosoever found him should not kill him' (Genesis 4:15). In a sense, then, Cain's de facto death sentence was commuted to a safer form of permanent exile ensured by some kind of physical sign. But what was this mysterious mark and what precisely did it communicate? Did it amount to a passport offering immunity? Did it betray the fact that Cain was being punished and if so, for what offense? Whatever the answers, Cain's branding (which was apparently painless) was integral to the process of punishment even if it did not amount to a discrete penal act. For the rest of his life Cain bore what sounds like a physical mark meant to identify him in a way that was immediately recognizable, even to strangers, as both protected and shunned by God. This form of personal labeling would become a technique of inclusive exclusion for many millennia to come.[82]

Cain's story is not only puzzling, it also provides a rare instance in the Jewish tradition of branding associated with a criminal act. Indeed, Leviticus 19:28, possibly echoing idolatrous practices, contains what amounts to a sweeping prohibition against any kind of permanent bodily marks (as distinct from circumcision), self-inflicted or otherwise: 'You shall not make gashes in your flesh for the dead, or incise any marks on yourselves: I am the Lord.' Mosaic and, later, Jewish law, however, certainly espoused corporal punishment via the early adoption of the *lex talionis*, a principle that, as we have seen, was not uncommon among earlier and contemporaneous civilizations: 'Eye for eye, tooth for tooth, hand for hand, foot for foot, burning for burning, wound for wound, stripe for stripe' (Exodus 21:24-25; and see Leviticus 24:19-20). Yet it is with particular respect to flogging that Jewish jurists stand out in terms of the attention they paid to it and the high degree to which they promoted its practice.[83] Their point of departure was the following passage from Deuteronomy (25:1-3):

> If people have a dispute, seek its resolution in court, and the judges render a decision in favor of the righteous one and condemning the wicked one; then, if the wicked one deserves to be flogged, the judge is to have him lie down and be flogged in his presence. The number of strokes is to be proportionate to his offense; but the maximum number is forty. He is not to exceed this; if he goes over this limit and beats him more than this, your brother will be humiliated before your eyes.

The principle of proportionality and a concern for obviating excess violence demonstrate that Jewish legislators were typical rather than unique in clarifying the conditions under which flogging was to be practiced. A peculiar twist however is that excess whipping was thought to result in humiliation or shaming, a notion that situates psychological anguish, rather than permanent physical damage or death, at the peak of pain's scale. Thus defined and regulated, flogging expanded throughout Late Antiquity and the Middle Ages. Operating under changing political fortunes and a generally declining autonomy, Jews turned flogging into a staple penalty as well as a form of disciplinary action. By the time of its completion in the early third century CE, the *Mishnah* sanctioned the use of penal whipping in no less than 168 cases, including transgression of dietary, agrarian, and Passover laws. The maximum number of blows was reduced to thirty nine, so as to avoid accidentally exceeding the sanctioned limit, and a preliminary physical examination was introduced to ascertain the culprit's capacity to sustain the blows, a condition that was reassessed at intervals during the act of flogging (*Makkot*).[84]

Some modern scholars have tried to set Jewish corporal punishment as relatively lenient and humane against the backdrop of reigning barbarism.[85] The shortcoming and typicality of such arguments should by now be clear. But there certainly was something particular about Jewish practices. In contrast to the biases of earlier and contemporaneous cultures, and possibly reflecting its limited political autonomy, Jewish law does not seem to have used flogging against any specific social or status group. This despite the claim by Flavius Josephus (*c.* 37-100 CE), who was likely influenced by a Greco-Roman tradition, that the measure is 'most ignominious' for a freeman.[86] While corporal punishment proliferated, however, measures such as capital punishment and *kerait* or death by divine intervention seem to have declined. Perhaps reflecting a greater need for social cohesion under gentile rule, the authors of the *Gemara* (3rd-5th centuries CE) and later commentators offered numerous exemptions from whipping, including commutation to a fine. Still, at least at the normative level, corporal punishment remained common throughout and beyond the Middle Ages. Maimonides (d. 1204), the highly influential medieval Jewish physician and legislator, dedicated three whole chapters in his *Mishneh Torah* (Sefer Shoftim, Sanhedrin 17-19) to enumerating 207 offenses punishable by stripes and to defining the terms of the measure's licit use.[87] By and large this discussion was integrated into Jewish Halacha through its reception by Joseph Karo's *Shulchan Aruch* (1563), which remains until this day the most authoritative prescriptive text in and beyond Orthodox Judaism.

Since the destruction of the Second Temple in the first century CE, rabbinic Judaism has been mostly a decentralized religion, its people living under varying degrees of cultural autonomy and religious tolerance, with very limited capacity (beyond excommunication) to enforce its own penal law.[88] Political transformations within the Jewish world, especially since the eighteenth century, brought even the semblance of a doctrinal unity to an end. And that, combined with Jews' lack of political autonomy, meant that relations between that religion and its numerous host states tended to be externally determined, and religious ideals of punishment, at least officially, remained minor sources of influence in the non-Jewish world. This does not exclude of course the possibility that corporal punishment was or continues to be practiced within certain tightly knit communities, be it in the domestic or semi-public sphere, but beyond anecdotal information the scale of the phenomenon is difficult to gauge. The Jewish State of Israel, whose penal code was mostly based on the British Criminal Code Ordinance of 1936, abolished corporal punishment from its penal code in 1950, that is two years after it gained independence, when corporal punishment for juveniles and prison inmates was still legal in Britain.[89]

Islam

Unlike their Jewish counterparts, early Islamic jurists dealt with punishment in general and corporal punishment in particular mostly within the context of a hegemonic culture; and in contrast with their Christian counterparts (who will be examined in the following section), they did so in the absence of an identifiable separation between church and state. These unique circumstances lend themselves to diverse interpretations of Sharia law's impact on promoting or curbing the use of bodily punishment, either by jurists' active participation or quietism or through their restricting of access to such penalties and devising alternative solutions. Supporting either extremity would require a certain amount of selectiveness, but perhaps not surprisingly it is especially observers seeking to decouple Islam and violence who employ corporal punishment as a cultural and political cudgel. If Muhammad's teachings are largely non-violent, scholars defending Islam's restraining effects on contemporary penal practices underscore Muslim rulers' departure from orthodoxy, as they 'began to acquire the tastes and vices of Greek and Persian emperors'.[90] The implication is that what was normal among foreigners was an aberration among Muslims, and numerous Muslim authors throughout the Middle Ages tried to scandalize their readers by reporting the flogging of an *amīr* or a scholar by (implicitly sacrilegious or outright deranged) Muslim rulers.[91] Needless to say, the ubiquity of such instances in the sources could and has been used as proof that corporal punishment was somehow particularly Islamic.

However one weighs the evidence, there is no doubt that Islamic scriptures, like those of Judaism and Zoroastrianism, condone corporal punishment. The Koran (mid-7th century CE) enjoins the use of corporal punishment, and especially flogging, on several occasions as either a mandatory (*hadd*) or a discretionary (*ta'zīr* and *siyāsa*) penalty for a range of offenses, including slander and sexual misconduct. Subsequent oral and written traditions, however, glossed and supplemented such verses, giving rise to different schools of interpretation. For instance, while Koran 24:2 states that a 'woman or man found guilty of sexual intercourse – lash each one of them with a hundred lashes', a later *hadīth* or oral tradition attributes to Muhammad a sentence of death by stoning against the woman and one hundred lashes and banishment for one year against the man.[92] And while Koran 5:90 prohibits the consumption of wine, a corporal penalty for drinking alcohol was only devised much later, also on the basis of an oral tradition.[93]

Islamic law's adoption of the *lex talionis* facilitated a selective use of dismemberment, although in some instances, especially under Shiite law, the penalty could be commuted into a fine, and there was a strict requirement to establish precisely what kind of physical damage had been incurred before retaliation could be ordered. In many cases the latter restriction closed the door on the possibility of legal retaliation.[94] Dismemberment was also prescribed in order to fulfill the goals of incapacitation and deterrence, as in the case of theft: '[As for] the thief, the male and the female, amputate their hands in recompense for what they committed as a deterrent [punishment] from Allah' (Koran 5:38). Last, Koran 5:33 lists cutting off the opposite hand and foot (cross-amputation) as one among several penalties that can be imposed upon anyone found guilty of corruption. Beyond these contexts corporal punishment in any form could be applied as a discretionary punishment whenever a defendant was awarded *ta'zīr*. Depending on the inclinations of a particular ruler and legal school, this could in theory be frequent, but in practice was subject to Islamic law's very strict rules of evidence and its desire to maintain bodily integrity, especially of the head, eyes, and genitalia, which were considered essential to one's personhood.[95]

Bodily integrity in particular came to impinge upon another form of corporal punishment, namely *tashhīr* or rendering someone infamous via public humiliation. Prescriptions and descriptions of such rituals from across the Islamicate world strongly suggest that culprits were routinely subjected to injury alongside verbal abuse, since executors burdened them physically in diverse ways and observers hurled objects at them or even beat them. More important, while such elements probably constituted abuses of a formal protocol, *tashhīr* could also involve shaving the culprit's head and blackening his or her face, measures that struck many Islamic jurists as a form of bodily mutilation (*muthla*). The conservative Hanbalī scholar Ibn

Qudāma (d. 1223), for instance, equated the blackening of faces to certain forms of facial dismemberment, an approach shared by followers of the Hanafi and Maliki schools as well.[96] Beyond demonstrating medieval Islamic jurists' sensitivity to questions of bodily integrity, such debates bring to light a form of corporal punishment that is (or at least can be) free from physical pain. Blackening the face is certainly an exception to the rule that corporal punishment and bodily pain go hand in hand, and yet jurists' focus on physical alteration suggests that, at least from a religious point of view, physical pain was subordinate to the location and kind of impairment or disability that ensued. The social and perhaps occupational consequences, in other words, were a paramount concern.

A related religious root of valuing bodily integrity (or a particular construction of that term) in Islam is the common association of physical blight with moral dubiousness, a link that has corollaries in Judaism and Christianity too (see also below).[97] Scholars have yet to establish whether under Islam people's attitudes towards disabled bodies was influenced by knowing what led to their present state. Yet there is little doubt that corporal punishment, along with war and disease, accounted for a substantial part of conditions associated with the Islamic category of ahl al-'āhāt or people of blights.[98] The social implications of certain disabilities were substantial, since non-impaired society considered those bearing them as prone to certain negative behaviors, on the one hand, and as subject to a different set of rules in the afterlife, on the other. Small wonder that major legal schools and scholars tried to limit recourse to punitive actions that, at least in part, could result in unnecessary stigmatization.[99]

There is little value in confronting superficial Western views of current Islamic legal culture with equally monochrome images of its past. Islamicate societies were many and diverse, a continuous state of affairs that manifested itself in their penal codes but perhaps especially in their punitive practices. The broad trends in corporal punishment's fortunes remain to be established for the period up to the Ottoman Empire and in different parts of the Islamic world. Suffice it to say that, at least in certain periods and regions, Muslims' limited recourse to corporal punishment actually set them apart from their European contemporaries. Around 1519, for instance, King Manuel I of Portugal was informed by one of his officials visiting North Africa that:

> [Corporal punishment] is not the habit of the Moors, for their only manner of punishment is through goods [...] it would be far worse for the Moors to see the ears being cut off a relative, or to see him being whipped, than to take away his whole fortune.[100]

Such observations, along with the legal provisions and debates discussed above, remind us that the links between Islam and corporal punishment are historical and contingent, not ideological and constant. As in Judaism, so in Islam, corporal punishment consolidated its prescriptive status as a staple penalty in the Middle Ages and so it remained throughout the early modern period, for instance under the Ottoman Empire. But once again we are nowhere near to knowing the extent to which it was practiced in these centuries. In some Muslim countries colonization by Western powers as well as independent state-building efforts brought pressure upon legislators and judges to mitigate corporal punishment by its commutation into fines, especially in the case of women, and by replacing penal amputation with incarceration. But it is far from clear whether these calls meant to address a perennial situation or rather more recent practices, to what extent they were successful, and what their relations were with local efforts at state building.[101] Today corporal punishments are administered in several Muslim countries, in some cases constituting an introduction of these measures (often imaged as a reintroduction) as recently as the 1980s.[102] But even among countries with a majority Muslim population, Saudi Arabia, Yemen, Sudan, northern Nigeria, Iran, and Pakistan are exceptional, not typical, in routinely applying corporal punishment in criminal procedures.[103]

Christianity

Christianity has been the world's largest religion for several centuries, laying claims to at least nominal adherence among one in three persons living today. As such it has influenced virtually all walks of human life, especially in Europe and the Americas, but also in large swathes of Africa and Asia. And yet, since for most of its history the Christian church has operated outside and at times as a counterweight to the secular political establishment, its direct contribution to penal law and practices specifically is less than obvious. In a sense, however, it was precisely this jurisdictional separation that allowed the church to develop its own penal code and apply it first and foremost among its own rank and file (priests, monks and nuns, and students) and to a lesser degree among the laity. Moreover, from a political and bureaucratic perspective, the Roman Catholic Church in particular has been a far more developed organization than its secular counterparts throughout most of its history, which explains how its activities remain on the whole better documented than those of most Late Antique, medieval and Renaissance courts. This allows us, as it did our predecessors, to observe some of its own blueprints for state building and disciplinary routines.

Within the context of these routines, corporal punishment occupies a marginal position, but perhaps not as marginal as is often thought. Early Christianity's blanket rejection of capital and corporal punishment (*sine vi humana*) in favor of, for instance, fines and incarceration, was to some extent at odds with hitherto prevailing notions of retributive justice, both Jewish and pagan. Yet bodily pain, let alone physical manipulation or alterations, did not disappear from the penal and disciplinary landscape altogether. Castration is a well-known case in point,[104] as is the penal tonsure forced upon secular leaders who fell from grace and were forced into monastic exile, their shorn heads imaging them as impotent.[105] But church leaders and, later, Canon lawyers also promoted the use of severe fasts, flagellation (also self-inflicted), sleep deprivation, and exposure to extreme weather conditions as licit ways to foster Christian identity and 'medicate' against sin. Among early medieval Irish monks, for instance, one text prescribes that:

> Simple contradiction of another's word is to be punished with fifty strokes; if out of contention, with an imposition of silence. If it is made in a quarrel, the penance should be for a week.

> If anyone, while washing lawfully in presence of his brethren, has done this standing [...] let him be corrected with twenty-four strokes.[106]

And according to another text:

> He who utters a vain word ought to be sentenced to silence for two hours thereafter or to twelve strokes;

> He who talks familiarly with a woman alone [...] shall remain without food or [do penance] for two days on bread and water, or [receive] two hundred strokes;

> He who speaks while eating, six blows. And he whose voice sounds from table to table, six blows. If it sounds outside from [within] the building, or from without sounds within, twelve strokes;

> For saying 'mine' or 'yours', six strokes;

> If he presumes to speak in the stated time of silence, without necessity, seventeen blows.[107]

3. The Flagellation of Christ.[111]

These and similar practices were originally developed among certain early Christian ascetics and in various monastic milieus, also as a way to emulate Christ's suffering (see fig. 3). Subsequently they were adopted by some lay people, at times residing in their original communities, at others living as lay penitents or oblates in monasteries.[108] In Ireland, for instance, commutations (*arrea*) included 'sleeping in waters, sleeping on nettles, sleeping on nut-shells, sleeping with a dead body in a grave, [and could be augmented by] sleep[ing] in cold churches or in secret chambers, performing vigil and praying without ceasing, viz. without sitting, without lying, without sleeping, as though they were in the mouth of hell'.[109] From the perspective of a Greco-Roman status-based penal tradition, there probably was something deeply humbling if not outright humiliating in free people's willingness to submit to physical pain; and this perspective was not lost on early Church leaders, who, on the one hand, construed such afflictions as a 'sweet inversion' of a pagan cultural taboo and, on the other, emphasized their continuity with a biblical tradition.[110]

Similar connections were made throughout Late Antiquity by Christian authors who described the bodily suffering of their brethren during periodic anti-Christian persecutions, traumatic spurts that entailed beating as well as forced prostitution.[112] Othering the non-Christian enemy as a persecutor characterized by a particular kind of brutality evoked such memories in later centuries, when Christianity as a whole was under reduced existential threat. For instance, the seventh-century *History of Vardan and the Armenian War* features two priests, Yovsēp and Levond, who are caned prior to their incarceration, and two confessors, Abraham and Khorēn, who are beaten and have their ears cut off before being enslaved.[113] Christian leadership, in other words, was expected to entail bodily pain and under certain circumstances even disfigurement. Saints from Stephen to Sebastian, following the example of Jesus, were depicted with the instruments and marks of their martyrdom. This may seem obvious from an iconographic perspective, but bodily disfigurement in Christianity, as in Islam, raised suspicions of sinfulness and criminality. Moreover, early Christian imaginations of the afterlife often presented the faithful's bodies intact, which urged theologians such as Augustine to explain the paradoxical situation whereby Christian martyrs appear to be less perfect than their unmarked coreligionists.[114]

Perhaps one response to these memories was clergymen's reluctance to practice corporal punishment in laymen's public spaces. Throughout the Middle Ages corporal punishment within the Church appears to have been mostly confined to the regular clergy (monks) and rarely practiced among the secular clergy (priests) unless the latter's punishment also involved cloistering. On the other hand, while the Church's capacity to apply its own range of penalties to lay people in this period varied widely across space and time,[115] at least some records suggest that corporal punishment was occasionally meted out as a main or additional sentence for a variety of offenses, especially as a form of discipline for children in and outside the classroom – and these were most often run by clerics.[116] Yet even in this realm, applying the rod was a considered measure, and authors theorizing about it often rejected staple Classical authorities on the matter in favor of distinguishing nuanced psychological attributes alongside the key role of pain in the economy of personal salvation.[117]

From a broader cultural perspective, then, the notion that sin and spiritual purgation involve physical pain and possibly impairment continued to have wide purchase among Catholic Christians. Likewise, the perceived causal relation between sin and divinely inflicted physical suffering in the afterlife endured, and was articulated and popularized throughout the Middle Ages, reaching an apogee of sorts in Dante Alighieri's *Comedy*, published in the early fourteenth century.[118] Applying the same logic, some laymen with particularly apocalyptic outlooks took to flogging themselves publically, the better to atone for their sins and those of their fellow men already in this life.[119] Secular regimes were also quick to harness the nexus of atonement through pain and depict public executions and corporal punishments in terms of Christ's Passion, without detracting from the culprit's guilt, while convicts manipulated their own procedures in ways that did, by appearing as humble penitents.[120] It was largely in response to this state of affairs that early Protestant thinkers such as Philipp Melanchthon (1497-1560) attempted to sever 'a link between mutilation, as a universal emblem of corporeal vulnerability and abjection, and holiness'.[121]

The end of Roman Catholic hegemony in sixteenth-century Europe, along with the rise of the Absolutist state, did not lead, as is often thought, to the overall separation of church and state and the contraction of religious law, including the regulation of corporal punishment. To begin with, secular and religious jurisdictions only partially overlapped in earlier eras, and even that area was routinely contested. Moreover, while the early modern period saw an increased policing of public morals by secular powers (the so-called criminalization of sin), it also witnessed an intensification of congregationally-based discipline, especially but not exclusively where state churches were absent, as in Scotland, Scandinavia, and the Dutch Republic.[122] Neither process entailed a significant change in the role of corporal punishment, despite criminal law's renewed commitment to bloodless penalties under Protestant influences. Flogging and the stocks, for instance, remained minor and thus largely stable measures employed in a Christian penal context.[123]

Medieval and Early Modern Europe

Medieval Europe is to the Western past what the Islamicate world is to the Western present: A foil to the achievements of modernity. Non-specialists commenting on virtually any topic, from gender to urban planning to medicine, and promoting nearly every current agenda imaginable, invoke the term 'medieval' not merely as a form of othering but as a downright pejorative. The Middle Ages have such a terrible reputation that, outside the field of medieval studies (and occasionally within it) people are willing to believe almost anything about that period, including fantasies such as that women wore chastity belts while their crusading husbands sojourned for months and even years abroad.[124] In the realm of punishment, medieval courts and rulers fall prey to allegations of arbitrariness and brutality, as they supposedly epitomize premodern penal modalities that focused on the body.[125] In Michel Foucault's influential (if hardly original) words, modernity began when '[t]he body as the major target of penal repression disappeared'.[126]

If we look at the numerous pertinent sources, however, the history of medieval and early modern European society's penal practices was less linear than is often thought, and recourse to corporal punishment specifically varied tremendously across space and time. Part of this fluctuation has to do with the political and legal diversity that characterized medieval Europe. While Europe grew increasingly more homogeneous since Late Antiquity in terms of institutional religion, it also experienced political fragmentation and fostered a concomitant legal pluralism. Different polities, occasionally conquering one another, operated under an array of traditions, including Roman and customary laws, which, juxtaposed with a more centralized Church, shaped a heterogeneous legal and penal landscape.[127]

Within this landscape, and contrary to a stereotypical view of medieval legal brutality, corporal punishment played a rather limited role.[128] Statistical analysis of medieval court records is mostly impossible before the thirteenth century due to a lack of sources, and remains complicated even thereafter. Still, according to a recent sampling of some well-documented Italian city-states, punishments were overwhelmingly pecuniary, and even the rare sentences of whipping and dismemberment that are attested were mostly issued against contumacious offenders (and thus were unlikely ever to be carried out) or could be commuted to fines or incarceration. Moreover, even this modest recourse to corporal punishment was in decline: From a combined rate of twenty-one percent (twenty-two out of one hundred and four cases) in the mid-fourteenth century, whippings declined by the mid-fifteenth century to three percent of all punishments (twenty-nine cases) and mutilation altogether disappeared.[129] In fact, contemporary distaste with such measures may already be detected in 1415, when Florentine lawmakers exiled the execution of corporal punishments to one thousand *bracchia* (roughly five hundred meters) beyond the city.[130]

To be sure, the wealth of Italy's criminal court records is exceptional, and the process they help trace is potentially unique within Europe. Yet the scattered evidence we do have, consisting of both descriptive and prescriptive sources, frustrates any attempt to trace a consistent decline in the use of flogging and dismemberment throughout the medieval period and in the transition from the late Middle Ages to early modernity. The statutes contained in *Rothair's Edict* (643), for instance, display a strong preference for monetary compensation according to social rank (*wergild*) and functional damage, while later collections of Norman and English law and descriptions of penal practices attest continually changing approaches but no general rejection of corporal punishment.[131] Early medieval Byzantium, by comparison, saw an unequivocal expansion of corporal punishment,[132] perhaps partly enabled by later Roman legislation on the matter, as we have seen. German and French customary laws such as the *Sachsenspiegel* (c. 1220) and Louis IX's *Etablissements* (c. 1254) likewise appear to have no qualms with dismemberment and branding, although there is some evidence to suggest that judges were being deterred from meting out bloody sentences.[133] Then again, among the Italian city-states in the fourteenth and fifteenth centuries, branding, amputations, and flogging were rare, and punishments tended to be overwhelmingly pecuniary,[134] while in England, by the mid-thirteenth century, mutilations practiced under Norman rule had all but disappeared, only to rise again to prominence under the Tudors in the late fifteenth and sixteenth centuries.[135]

The latter trend found a chronological parallel in the Netherlands, where branding and, more commonly, whipping (with an average of roughly forty stripes per punishment) were carried out both secretly and (increasingly) in public, often accompanied by exposure on the scaffold.[136] Throughout the Habsburg Empire, the enacted *Constitutio Criminalis Carolina* (c. 1532) paved the way for increased use of judicial torture and corporal punishment (§§101, 104, 196-198), as was the wont of ever more powerful monarchs in contemporary France.[137] In Britain, as Humanism, the Reformation, and early modernity began to set in, Henry VIII's Whipping Act of 1530 expanded the use of flogging against vagrants, shaping the country's summary justice system for many years to come. According to one study:

> Throughout the sixteenth and seventeenth centuries, men and women were sentenced to be whipped at Quarter Sessions for an immense variety of offenses. Not only rogues

and vagabonds, but the mothers of illegitimate children, Scottish pedlars, beggars, drunkards, fortune tellers, sex offenders and even lunatics were all flogged for their crimes and misfortunes.[138]

And back in the Netherlands, branding remained licit and apparently fairly common under both Habsburg and French rules, until it was banned in 1854.[139] In short, the image of medieval rulers' frequent use of corporal punishment is a gross generalization at best, and the association of early modernity with a decline in such penalties is patently false. Indeed, it is plausible that European societies during the two centuries preceding the Enlightenment and the birth of modern penology experienced a higher level of standardization and a subsequent increase in recourse to corporal punishment than the barbarous Middle Ages.

In terms of how corporal punishment was employed and what political and other elites sought to communicate through it, studies of late-medieval French and Dutch practices suggest the presence of both indexing and mimesis. In France, branding the forehead of a thief (*voleur*) with a V or that of an able-bodied pauper (*mendiant*) with an M was routine, as was burning the lips and tongues of blasphemers. Thieves could have their arms as well as their ears amputated, thereby combining both ironic talion and indexing, as the former measure ostensibly punishes the offending member and the latter labels the culprit in a different way.[140] In the Low Countries it was common practice among secular rulers (with, presumably, the tacit support of the Church) to brand heretics or those who offended the Church with a cross on the forehead, and merchants who falsified their city's arms were branded with those very same icons. Another form of ironic branding in the sixteenth century was to mark the cheek of a bigamist with an image of a distaff (a feminine symbol at that time),[141] and those convicted by secular courts for having 'offended with their tongue' (lying, defaming, inciting rebellion, as well as blaspheming) could have it burned, pierced, or removed, a practice also attested for Scotland.[142] Last, in early modern Denmark, landlords flogged peasants fixed to a wooden horse, in a gesture that was universally seen as degrading, perhaps due to the animalization it entailed.[143]

None of this is to argue that corporal punishment, and dismemberment in particular, was so commonly employed that it lost its tremendous shock value.[144] Defacing punishments such as eye-gouging and nose-cutting, to take two prominent examples, were closely associated with dehumanizing/animalizing and thus proved especially effective in delegitimizing political and religious authority (notably but not exclusively in Byzantium, with its long tradition of blinding and castrating former or would-be political elites).[145] Yet dismemberments were also variously employed at different times and regions. Under King Edgar (r. 959-975), for instance, nose-cutting was the prescribed fate of thieves, but during Cnut the Great's rule (1016-1035) it became a staple punishment for female adulterers.[146] In late-medieval German cities, by contrast, there was a move away from mirroring crimes by punishments, but severed human hands came to symbolize the practice of state power and were preserved as judicial mementos as well as used by critics of that power to parody its judicial process.[147] Corporal punishment could be gendered in other ways than those already suggested. In the fifteenth-century Low Countries, for example, gender determined whether or not a convicted offender would be exposed on the pillory (men) or obliged to carry stones (women), although in practice there was some overlap between the outcomes.[148]

Finally, socioeconomic status or a culprit's financial means as well as race or simply foreignness could play an important role in shaping his or her corporal punishment. As in antiquity, so in the Middle Ages, domestic servants (who were often foreigners and non-Christians) and children could be beaten with impunity (also at school),[149] and non-citizens on the whole fared worse with regard to public executions, shaming, and corporal punishment.[150] Moreover, there is some evidence from the late Middle Ages regarding the conversion of corporal penalties into monetary fines

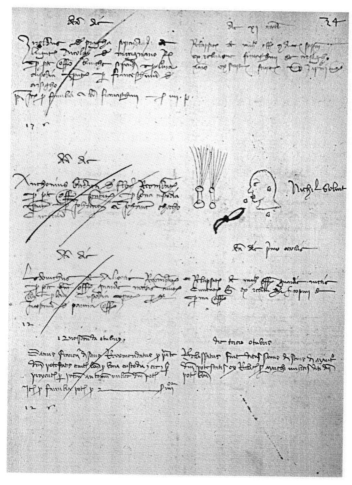

4. Flogging and dismemberment of a medieval prisoner.

and vice versa. As the image above suggests, corporal punishment could be the fate of offenders who were fined beyond their means.

In this case, a creative prison scribe in Bologna possibly illustrated the fate of Antonio Benedetti, an inmate whose original punishment was likely a monetary fine or else he owed money to a private individual. He did not, would not, or could not pay the required sum ('nichil solvit') and was subsequently subjected to flogging and dismemberment, as the image suggests he lost his tongue and an ear and was then released (otherwise he would not appear in the column marking prison exits). The significance of the evidence of such practices, which is mostly French and Italian, is ambiguous. It may suggest a prescriptive swing away from corporal punishment, but it may also indicate a class bias in the application of such commutations: Those who could afford to pay, remained intact, while those who could not, did not. In other words, in certain contexts certain bodily marks would brand a person as belonging to a lower socioeconomic status rather than as merely a criminal.

The Middle Ages, a period out of which Western civilization was allegedly reborn, having rejected many of its shared assumptions and values, is hard to typify in terms of princely rulers' or urban regimes' recourse to corporal punishment. On the one hand, diverse evidence from this long era strongly suggests that, as in preceding periods, court-issued corporal punishment as well as the measure's use in private settings is difficult to shoehorn into a particular mold. On the other, and as the next and final section will demonstrate, modern societies in and beyond Europe continued to practice corporal punishment, and in certain cases even expanded its use. In this sense, the period known as early modernity did indeed operate as a watershed moment in the history of corporal punishment, but in ways that depart from its traditional image. As we shall see, from a global perspective, European corporal punishment achieved a renaissance of sorts with the expansion of European powers into the Americas, Africa, and Asia.

Modernity to the Present

The evidence surveyed in the previous section undermines a prevalent view, especially outside specialist circles, that associates the demise of corporal punishment with the West's transition into modernity. Moreover, it implies that Enlightenment figures such as Cesare Beccaria (1738-1794) and Jeremy Bentham (1748-1832), the founding fathers of modern penology, developed their reformist blueprints in response to the specific penal practices of the early modern period rather than to any perennial premodern state of affairs.[151] Whatever the immediate backdrop to their interventions had been, these theorists rejected corporal measures as both inequitable in their execution and ineffectual in promoting remorse and behavioral change. Instead, they favored what they argued was the more precise and disciplining regime of incarceration, a penal modality that eventually – even if temporarily – achieved a broad consensus in Western countries. In its numerous local and regional applications this process, often known as 'the birth of the prison', is a familiar if incomplete story.[152]

It is more an assumption than a conclusion of existing prison histories that the development of penal incarceration in Europe and elsewhere came at the expense of corporal punishment, at least *outside* the prison.[153] Even putting aside the physical risks and hardships that imprisonment entailed and continues to pose, as well as the bodily ramifications of ostensibly non-physical punishments such as fines, it is emphatically not the case that the prison buried the whip, be it in theory, policy, or practice. Bentham himself, it is often forgotten, not only designed the famous Panopticon, but also proposed – in the very same treatise – to reduce arbitrariness in punishment as follows:[154]

A machine might be made, which should put in motion certain elastic rods of cane or whalebone, the number and size of which might be determined by the law: the body of the delinquent might be subjected to the strokes of these rods, and the force and rapidity with which they should be applied, might be prescribed by the Judge [...] A public officer, of more responsible character than the common executioner, might preside over the infliction of the punishment; and when there were many delinquents to be punished, his time might be saved, and the terror of the scene heightened, without increasing the actual suffering.

Enlightenment and later thinkers' overlooked tolerance of physical punishment was reflected in policy and practice as well, both in and beyond Europe. In his proposed reform of Virginia's penal code, for instance, Thomas Jefferson (1743-1826) envisaged that 'no crime shall be henceforth punished by the deprivation of life and limb', but hastened to add a number of important exceptions. A man convicted of rape, sodomy, or polygamy, for instance, would be castrated, while a woman convicted of similar crimes would be punished 'by boring through the cartilage of her nose a hole of one half inch in diameter at the least'. Anyone intentionally disfiguring another 'shall be maimed or disfigured in like sort; or if that cannot be, for want of the same part, then as nearly as may be, in some other part'.[155]

The principles of the *lex talionis* evidently survived yet another alleged sea change, and along with physical measures such as forced labor, continued to feature in contemporary and later Western penal regimes.[156] To offer two examples, the leading Italian criminologist of his generation, Cesare Lombroso (1835-1909), proposed to treat certain minor offenders away from prisons and with cold showers and restricted diets, regimes explicitly cited as corporal measures,[157] while contemporary Dutch parliaments continued to debate how to regulate corporal punishment *inside* prisons, where flogging would remain in vogue for several decades.[158] Moreover, increasingly democratic as well as colonial regimes frequently applied corporal measures in various contexts deep into the twentieth century. A broad historical perspective, in other words, exposes once again the fallacy that penology is a zero-sum game, and illustrates that, alongside prisons' undeniable proliferation since the nineteenth century,[159] the supposed decline of corporal punishment has been – if anything – remarkably slow, and remains far from complete, even with the rise of the modern democratic nation-state. Indeed, one could argue that it was precisely the latter process of political centralization that added so much space for new and complex penal systems to grow, without forcing older practices entirely into retirement.

There are a number of explanations why Enlightenment-era calls to abolish corporal punishment took time to gain traction and to be translated, however partially, into practice. As we have just seen, even the new philosophers of punishment were not united on this front. Moreover, given how deeply engrained earlier measures were, it is small wonder that skeptical voices across Europe warned against mayhem, especially as regards juvenile delinquency. Even the most supportive regimes found it difficult to build and maintain the momentum for penal reform, as the pendulum of public and professional opinion continued to swing between the abolition and the expansion of corporal punishment.

It is against this background – a tug-of-war rather than an unfolding linear process – that historical and anthropological works on corporal punishment in this period proliferated. Illuminating past and present societies' recourse to whipping, branding, and dismemberment both celebrated a nascent promise and projected apprehension about its future. Works such as Jean-Denis Lanjuinais' *La bastonnade et la flagellation pénales considérées chez les peuples anciens et chez les modernes* (1825; repr. 1879), H.M.M. Pape's *Ueber die Wiedereinführung der Prügelstrafe und die Züchtigung des Gesindes* (1853), Augustin Cabanès' *Flagellation in France from a Medical and Historical Standpoint* (1898; repr. 1901), Charles Norton Barney's *Circumcision and Flagellation among the Filipinos* (1903), Pierre Guénolé's *L'étrange passion: la flagellation dans les mœurs d'aujourd'hui* (1904), and E. Bussler's *Die Prügelstrafe* (1906), among others, were composed in a deeply polemical context and were partly engaged in essentializing, exoticizing, and othering users of corporal punishment, thereby setting up the measure as a litmus test for a country's (often *their* country's threatened) degree of civilization. It was in this period too that James Glass Bertram's pseudonymous and enormously popular *A History of the Rod*

(1840; 2nd ed. 1869; repr. 1870; 1873; 1877; 1910; 1969; 2002), discussed in the Introduction, began its long and successful career, and when Jacques Boilleau's much earlier work, *Historia flagellantium* (1700; French translation 1701), was successfully relaunched in English under the title *History of Flagellation among Different Nations* (1888; repr. 1903; 1920; 1952; 1964). Among Europeans, what drove this trend is more likely a mixed fear of and excitement about corporal punishment's impending return, rather than a sense of its inevitable demise.

Indeed, at least some of these authors were reacting directly to current affairs. The idiosyncratic politician and polymath Lanjuinais, for instance, begins his study with the somewhat misleading assertion that 'caning [*la bastonnade*] did not exist in France before 1789, neither in law nor in usage', and implies that its recent proliferation within France is precipitating the kingdom (!) headlong into barbarism.[160] Opponents of corporal punishment in England likewise had much to fear from the issuing of several Bills, beginning with the Security from Violence Act (1863). This law expanded the use of flogging against certain offenses substantially, and its apparent success generated further calls to reinstate a penalty that had almost been abolished by then.[161] By World War I, Henry Salt, representing the Humanitarian League, felt compelled to issue an alarming report entitled *The Flogging Craze*, in which he characterized flogging and its expansion as (inevitably) 'a return to a mediæval punishment'. Echoing earlier critics and foreshadowing later ones, he presented the advocacy of flogging as being 'associated, in a peculiar degree, with anger, passion, and the inability to listen rationally to the dictates of logic and experience'.[162] A generation later, R.G. van Yelyr expressed his concern about flogging, namely that 'a considerable as well as a powerful section [of the British public] is in favour of an *extension* of this form of punishment'.[163] In this way, on either side of the Channel and throughout the nineteenth, early and mid-twentieth century, corporal punishment continuously reemerged as a cudgel to fight at least a perceived if not a real threat.

Beyond the turbulent home front, European corporal punishment had a new, global context. Both before and after nineteenth-century reforms prompted a reshaping of Europe's penal landscape, Western colonial powers abroad remained quite tolerant and often enthusiastic about using corporal punishment among indigenous populations throughout Africa, Asia, and the Americas.[164] As we have already seen for parts of Asia and North Africa, local practices of corporal punishment varied widely over time even within the same civilizations. And the picture becomes no less complicated as we turn our attention briefly to the Americas. The Aztecs, for instance, inflicted diverse offenders with painful forms of capital punishment, but other than shaming penalties such as shaving a culprit's head, corporal punishment by itself was virtually unknown.[165] Likewise among the Maya, other than an isolated reference to ear-cutting for convicted thieves and adulterers (augmented by cutting off the hands of the former in grave cases) in what is now Honduras, corporal punishment was rare.[166] Further north, English and French colonists encountered what they often self-righteously described as heinous torture (including branding) among the semi-nomadic Hurons, Algonquin, and Iroquois, although such acts were not necessarily penal. They could for instance take place in the context of private vengeance as well as requickening (the ritual bestowing of a new life to an aggrieved party) and adoption.[167] Similar descriptions of war captives running the gauntlet were likewise presented as punishment although the act was likely meant to test the men's courage or simply used as a form of (admittedly cruel) amusement.[168] Most of those convicted for all but treason and witchcraft, offenses that could lead to a death penalty, either had their property destroyed or atoned by offering gifts to the victim or his or her family or clan, as seems to have been typical among numerous traditional societies.[169] One exception among the Iroquois was shaving an adulteress's hair as a way to shame her (another case in which gender skewed punishment), but otherwise corporal punishment for theft (as well as burning at the stake and certain forms of torture) appear to have post-dated Europeans' arrival.[170]

Compared with its limited use by indigenous peoples, flogging and branding flourished among colonizers and under colonial rules in both North and South America. According to a recent survey, in New England 'most settlements had a public whipping and pillory for inflicting serious physical pain and public humiliation' upon deviant settlers. For the southern colonies, the authors aver that such practices abated somewhat after 1800, but their comment that '[p]ublic whippings were increasingly restricted to particular contexts (e.g. military punishments, disobedience by slaves)', seems to marginalize the penal fate of rather a substantial part of the country's population.[171] In Georgia, for instance, flogging was the second most common penalty inflicted by the state (that is, beyond the routine penal activities in the plantations) on black slaves between 1755 and 1850, and it remained a frequent measure thereafter as either a single punishment or in combination with branding (A for arson, B for burglary, M for murder) and transportation. Along with the rise of slaves' monetary value and the decline of their capital punishment, the average and median number of lashes in Georgia rose markedly between the colonial and the antebellum periods, from 123/75 to 220/195.[172] For black slaves, in sum, neither the Enlightenment nor Independence presented a watershed moment as far as corporal punishment was concerned; indeed, even the Civil War could not bring such practices to an end, as the country's economic integration made forced (and often lethal) convict labor and its attendant corporal discipline highly attractive pursuits for state and corporate coffers.[173] The same holds, albeit to a lesser extent, for Southern whites, whose punishments became less severe physically as the nineteenth century progressed. However, whipping remained a very common penalty for poor whites in this period, and could be meted out singularly or in combination with being held in stocks, branding, and banishment.[174]

In central and south America too, race and status set apart those more likely from those less likely to receive sentences of corporal punishment. In colonial Mexico during the mid-eighteenth and early nineteenth centuries, for example, mestizos and mulattoes were twice as likely as Spaniards and Indians to incur flogging in addition to their prison sentences, which otherwise tended to be of equal length.[175] In Argentina during the same period, the legal system was similarly prone to afflicting *gente de color* with flogging as an additional sentence.[176] And in Brazil (as elsewhere), where color converged with status, non-free men (mostly blacks) were the only major group not exempt from corporal punishment outside the army well into the nineteenth century.[177]

Colonial practices of corporal punishment, then, under-scored and perpetuated both racial status and socioeconomic marginality even as similar measures were being curbed (but hardly eliminated) back home, or at least construed by some learned elites as degenerate. The irony is most apparent among indigenous peoples who came under colonial regimes, but othering can be documented among lower-status European immigrants and migrating laborers and slaves. Daily life aboard the ships of the Dutch East Indies Company (a de facto state subsidiary), for instance, involved much flogging, branding, piercing, and the so-called keelhaul as legitimate and common punishments, despite or perhaps due to their tendency to result in death.[178]

British immigrants to Australia, some with a criminal background, many others socioeconomically and geographi-cally marginal back home, were routinely subjected to corporal punishment, a practice that lasted in institutional and domestic contexts well into the twentieth century.[179] In India, corporal punishment was promoted and then abolished under the Brit-ish in 1834, only to be restored by the very same regime thirty years later, allegedly in order to deal with mutinies.[180] Here too, while the rod's status may have been (temporarily) declining back home, exporting it was booming business. In this way too colonial penal policies left a long shadow, and while some former

5. Keelhauling from aboard a Dutch ship.

colonies and protectorates chose to eradicate them, others maintained and even promoted their use. Israel, with its European-trained legal elites and a relatively short experience of British rule, struck corporal punishment from its penal code within two years of declaring independence in 1948, while judicial caning in Singapore, Malaysia, and Brunei, which likewise can be traced back at least to British rule, has become both a mandatory and a discretionary penalty for numerous offenses, and its application has accordingly experienced a sharp rise since decolonization.[181]

Thus, in what was either wishful thinking, a grossly inaccurate observation, or a hackneyed othering statement, George Ryley Scott concluded in 1938 that, '[a]part from exceptional cases, penal flogging has disappeared from civilization'.[182] From a broader perspective, corporal punishment continued to play a prominent role as a main, additional, or *sub rosa* penalty in numerous countries, while in others they have been only recently banned. In England and Wales, for instance, corporal punishment *outside* prisons and juvenile institutions was abolished only in 1948, and remained a divisive issue among criminal justice professionals for decades.[183] In Kenya, the already practiced penalty of whipping was extended in 1945 to apply to convicted burglars, and across the Atlantic, flogging was introduced against crop thieves in Jamaica in 1942. In Trinidad, corporal punishment was abolished in 1941 but reintroduced several years later.[184] Meanwhile, these and similar laws have been suppressed, but the process has been slow, not least in the US. In 1952, the last documented public whipping in the West's largest democracy took place in Delaware, but the law allowing it remained on the books until 1972. Meanwhile, a very modern form of corporal punishment, namely chemical castration (which is potentially painless and theoretically reversible), has been introduced as a mandatory measure against certain repeat sexual offenders by state legislators in California and Florida, and is practiced in seven other US states as well as periodically in Argentina, India, Israel, Russia, and South Korea. Needless to say, critics present this modern intervention, which relies on advanced medical research, as a return to the Middle Ages.[185]

There are other indications for the longevity of corporal punishment, which, as we have seen, for thousands of years has been a staple of summary justice and discipline in the semi-public and professional spheres, to say nothing of the private and domestic ones. Child psychologists and psychiatrists employ the term corporal punishment today mostly to the chagrin of crime and punishment scholars,[186] who argue that transgressions in these environments rarely constitute crimes and consequently their deserts cannot be construed as punishments. That is to say, whipping a child for uttering profanities is a disciplinary measure meant to foster a certain behavioral norm that may or may not be strongly frowned upon outside the school or home; and slapping a spouse for sexual infidelity has less to do with enforcing a law than with expressing shame or frustration over broken promises or unmet expectations. Conversely, and in keeping with the treatment of slaves in earlier periods, the laws of many countries do not regard such measures as a form of summary justice.[187]

Yet campaigns for the abolition of corporal punishment find it not only inherently important but also strategically useful to focus on children's rights and the domestic sphere. For despite their different goals and dynamics, child rearing and criminal justice are related in significant ways. Disciplinary action in domains such as the home and the school and in religious and vocational institutions both reflects and extends mechanisms, procedures, and power structures in the world outside.[188] Corporal punishment at home, for instance, can help legitimize and perpetuate corporal punishment outside. As one case study concludes:

> If Victorian fathers were prepared to beat their own children, it followed that they would be prepared to have them whipped at school. It also followed that they would be likely to approve of the judicial flogging of juvenile offenders. But the British (and especially the English) did not leave it at that: they flogged adults too. The English Vice began in the home, spread to the home's most obvious extension, the school (particularly the boarding school), and thence to the courts, the prison, the Army and Navy, the colonies – and the brothels. The British Empire, it might be argued, was founded on the lash.[189]

Such processes in Britain and elsewhere may have been more than unidirectional, of course. But it is undeniable that non-public disciplinary action, including the use of corporal punishment, offers a political education and helps shape new generations' ideas of licit and illicit violence, hierarchies, and desired power relations in the world around them. Conversely, penalties meted out by the state are often in tune with those employed in domestic, religious, and professional contexts. In other words, so long as this cycle remains unbroken, it is unlikely that pain will be excised from either legal penalties or domestic discipline, rendering the very recent consensus on the need to protect children from disciplinary violence, be it at home or in school, more apparent than real.[190] At the normative level, as of January 2014, only thirty-five countries offer children full legal protection from corporal punishment.[191] And while most of the latter are Western, it seems that despite no lack of local and global advocacy efforts, societies in which corporal punishment is applied to children with impunity remain the rule, not the exception.[192]

The prevalent use of non-judicial corporal punishment (spanking, belting, slapping, but also diverse forms of deprivation) in many milieus, then, needs to be understood in its broadest cultural terms. Rather than reduce this state of affairs in the West to a sign of immigrant maladjustment or attribute it to psychopathologies, such penal practices can also be seen as an enduring toleration and in some cases growing appreciation of physical pain as a legitimate aspect of discipline and the promotion of social order, dating back to Classical Greece and Ancient Rome.[193] In many present-day Western societies the use of physical force by authority figures remains a battleground for competing truth claims about discipline, morality, and cultural legitimacy. Despite consistent and growing evidence of routine spanking's adverse short-, medium-, and long-term effects on children's mental health,[194] there is no shortage of parents and guardians who continue to advocate it for two main reasons: First, spanking is irresistibly effective; children generally respond to it (or its threat) quickly. Secondly, it is tolerated, condoned, or outright encouraged by numerous (ancient, medieval, and modern) authorities in the domestic, academic, and religious spheres.

To state the obvious, such authorities in the West are hardly limited to those following Sharia law or influenced by Islamic culture. Among those drawing inspiration from the Old Testament, some continue to hold literally that 'He who spares the rod, hates his child' (Proverbs 13:24).[195] Cultural but not necessarily religious conservatives exhibit a similar attitude. The ban on corporal punishment in British 'public' schools, for instance, was voted into law only as recently as 1998 and by a narrow majority at that. And in the US, where bans on corporal punishment date back some one hundred and fifty years, 'padding' remains the default prerogative of schools in some twenty states, despite an apparent consensus that '[h]itting children in school does not help them achieve academic success [...] Instead, they feel humiliated, helpless, depressed, and angry'.[196] To these persistent forces countering the rod's demise in homes and schools – and by implication in the public sphere – one must add an even wider faith in violence as a legitimate means to resolve disputes, the right to maintain privacy, and religious and cultural autonomy. As we edge into the twenty-first century, the high regard in which numerous Western societies continue to hold each of these principles strongly suggests that corporal punishment is alive and kicking. This may be reassuring news for advocates of corporal punishment, however limited the scale with which they wish to apply it may be. Conversely, those who strive for a world where such measures are a thing of the past, have little reason to be complacent.

Finally, two recent developments may help corporal punishment remain at a safe distance from history's dustbin. Growing discontent with the US prison system has led some criminal justice scholars to advocate the reintroduction of corporal punishment – electrocution and flogging, in particular – into the penal system as a morally superior as well as efficient substitute for or an alternative to incarceration.[197] Such proposals are generally seen as provocative and do not define the mainstream of present-day penology, at least not yet. But their advocates are genuinely concerned professional observers, who express at least in part the criticisms and desired solutions of others, exasperated as they are with a broken and hugely expensive system. If their proposals ultimately gain traction, we may witness a veritable surge in what is commonly understood as corporal punishment, an 'unantici-pated turn' in penal history. The second development concerns sentences of public notice, which expose culprits who must identify themselves as sex offenders, drunk drivers, or domestic abusers, to discrimination, abuse, and even physical violence.[198] This, along with accessible Web-based criminal registries and the proliferation of social media, may precipitate a rise in new kinds of virtual and physical bullying and public shaming protocols that, informally but not altogether unintentionally, could lead to extra-legal bodily harm, as we have seen happen in the past.[199]

With all this in mind, to argue, as Steven Pinker has recently done, that '[i]n the modern West and much of the rest of the world, capital and corporal punishments have been effectively eliminated', is to ignore a still salient aspect of Western penal practices.[200] As David Garland has shown, modern, systematic penology may have encouraged a rethinking of the link between physical pain and punishment, but it has hardly been able to sever the two.[201] On the other hand, it is far from clear that bodily suffering was perennially central to premodern punishment or that bodily pain is always and everywhere coextensive with corporal punishments, with their semiotic subtleties and long-term communicative goals. The allegedly premodern focus on the body as a deviant territory that requires disciplining may have only expanded with the rise of scientific criminology, the rationalization of state apparatuses, and modern medicine.[202] And from a still broader cultural perspective, bodily trauma retains (and according to some observers has even expanded) its place in present-day society through diverse media.[203] In sum, modern societies inflicting bodily pain on convicted criminals or simply seeking to inscribe their values upon their deviants' bodies as a form of punishment can be understood in the broader terms of penal history's ebbs and flows.

Conclusion

In 2007, the Malaysian government released a crime-fighting video showcasing its treatment of major offenders. The culprit in question was a convicted drug dealer, who was sentenced to long-term incarceration and twenty blows with a *rotan*, a punishment illustrating how a supposedly staple premodern and an emblematic modern mode of punishment continue to coexist.[204] The images of the caning session are vivid and disturbing. With effort, I watched through to the fourth blow, but other viewers evidently found the experience less taxing, judging by the nearly 400,000 views it has logged so far. Either way, scrolling down the hundreds of written reactions offers a sobering reminder of how undecided the matter of corporal punishment remains across the globe, and why. Crass jokes and sexual innuendo aside ('in Malaysia it's a punishment, in San Francisco it's a lifestyle choice'), most comments ran the gamut from utter revulsion ('animals!') to wholehearted approval. Among the latter – heirs to a strong tradition of Virtue flogging Vice – not a few, ostensibly Western, responders considered what they just saw as a potentially useful way to fight crime on the streets and improve discipline at home: 'We need this in Europe'; 'I wish our local PD would do this for all the little punks caught burglarizing homes and stealing stereos'; 'A measure designed to deter illegal immigrant workers. Sounds good to me. How about also for CEO's who outsource your jobs to third world countries as well??'

To readers of the foregoing pages, the alternating acceptance and rejection of such practices among Western commentators should come as no surprise. What could also be expected at this juncture are the terms in which genuine shock and horror were expressed ('Brutal, savage, primitive and immoral') and how quickly some of the comments moved to characterize the event as symptomatic of a non-human society ('monkeys') or a deviant civilization, especially when several viewers pointed out that the video hails from Malaysia, a Muslim country, rather than

Singapore, as the title caption incorrectly announces. Although both Malaysia and Singapore are, from a certain Western perspective, far-flung former colonies, the latter can be construed as an exotic quasi-Western outpost, whereas the former can more easily succumb to the label of a religious and cultural other. To quote the very mildest responses posted in this vein: 'Muslims beating muslims. Fine with me'; 'what a shit-hole. Filled with barbaric idiots. No wonder the British gave it back to em'; 'This is Malaysia and they are muslims. It is the will of allah that one mans bare buttocks shalt be smitten by another muslim, whilst a bunch more muslims stand round watching.' That penal flogging was introduced to, or at any rate routinely practiced in Malaysia by the British lies too deep in the background, as does the fact that the country's Sharia law courts – whatever their specific approach to corporal punishment may be – are largely subordinate to the country's common law courts and do not deal with criminal matters.[205]

More important, however, is the respondents' commonly shared assumption about a clear divide between cultures and nations that do and those that do not apply corporal punishment. As we have seen, corporal punishment is scarcely a marginal phenomenon, straddling not only a non/Western divide today, but a pre/modern one generally. Nonetheless, its representation as a form of atavism continues to function, as it has for the past millennia and in a variety of earlier societies, as a cultural and political cudgel. However false, the dichotomy remains effective, largely owing to the accessibility of two registers corporal punishment operates in, marking internal deviants and external others. Both have ensured that human bodies remain a significant site of the Western penal landscape well into modernity.

Acknowledgments

Only a medievalist could have written this book. Or so I was led to believe by a commissioning editor who, back in 2011, asked me to contribute an encyclopedia entry on the history of corporal punishment. The fact that I hadn't published anything on the topic did not seem to matter; I had written a book on medieval prisons and that was close enough. Besides, medievalists should know about such things since flogs, like the plague, were always in the air during the Middle Ages. I embraced my essentialized identity and proceeded with the project. Time and space meant that only a fraction of what I discovered made it into the original essay,[206] and as I continued to expand my source base, my approach to the topic changed, as did my understanding of penal history in general and corporal punishment itself. I can now appreciate even better why I was asked to write that essay and why that was at the same time deeply – and typically – misguided.

In other words, only a medievalist could *not* have written this book. Indeed, it took a small global village, including Pepijn Brandon, Haran Fainstein, Roy Flechner, Moritz Föllmer, James Kennedy, Christian Lange, Ruud Peters, Kristina Richardson, Petra Sijpesteijn, Ofer Sitbon, Patricia Skinner, Daniel Lord Smail, Yael Sternhell, Paul Stephenson, Jonathan Stökl, Fritz Umbach, and Michiel van Groesen to compensate, however partially, for my ignorance and make this book a feasible endeavor. I am deeply grateful to them all and to Frans Camphuijsen, David Garland, Mary Gibson, Shelly Makleff, Pieter Spierenburg, and Neslihan Şenocak for their critical comments on earlier drafts, and to Claire Weeda, who rendered the original text into Dutch. I would also like to record my appreciation to the individuals, museums, archives, and libraries that permitted us to reproduce the accompanying images, to the University of Amsterdam for giving me the opportunity to teach and research the topic, and to Brooklyn and the Villa I Tatti, for providing a space to write about it. Simon Forde lassoed this project and led it into the Amsterdam University Press barn, where Marjolijn Voogel ably transformed one text into two books.

Brooklyn / Amsterdam / Villa I Tatti
August 2014

Notes

1. Resnik and Curtis, 'Representing Justice'. For a non-Western perspective see Mariottini Spagnoli, 'The Symbolic Meaning of the Club'; and Glucklich, 'The Royal Scepter (*Danda*)'.

2. On selfing and othering see Schor, 'This Essentialism Which is Not One'.

3. Smith, *Punishment and Culture*, 171.

4. A similar if more limited function of punishment, almost inevitably corporal, is typical of diverse vertebrates. See Clutton-Brock and Parker, 'Punishment in Animal Societies'. On humans afflicting animals with corporal punishment see Girgen, 'The Historical and Contemporary Prosecution of Animals', at 112-113, 121, and 124.

5. Pinker, *The Better Angels of Our Nature*. In part, Pinker's observation is based on a tendentious reading of scholars, such as Pieter Spierenburg, who have successfully documented a decline in certain kinds of violent crimes and physical punishments since the early modern era. Many of these studies assume rather than illustrate that physical brutality in crime and punishment must have been more widespread in earlier and less well-documented periods, and therefore go to great lengths to explain modern 'remnants' of such practices as aberrations. See Spierenburg, *Violence and Punishment*.

6. Armchair histories such as Sperati, 'Amputation of the Nose Throughout History', are hardly unique in this sense, as we shall see.

7. Filkins, 'The Thin Red Line', 46. See also Naipaul, *Among the Believers*, 81, 92, 164-169, 289, 391, and 399.

8. An exceptional flurry of condemnations descended upon Singapore in 1994, when an eighteen-year-old American, Michael P. Kay, was sentenced to four months' incarceration, a 3,500 Singapore Dollar fine, and twelve lashes for theft and vandalism. It was probably the first and so far the last such outcry from the international community. A more recent flogging sentence involving a Swiss citizen, Oliver Fricker (also convicted of vandalism), was greeted mostly with silence.

9. Moskos, *In Defense of Flogging*, 147 (italics original).

10. Newman, *Just and Painful*.

11. Hibbert, *The Roots of Evil*, 411.

12. Douglas, *Purity and Danger*, 143.

13. Elias, *The Civilizing Process*.

14. Durkheim, 'Two Laws of Penal Evolution'.

15. Cooper, *Flagellation and the Flagellants*; later revised and published as *A History of the Rod in all Countries: From the Earliest Period to the Present Time* (London: William Reeves, 1877 [repr. 1898]); reprinted as *An Illustrated History of the Rod* (London: Wordsworth, 1988); and most recently under the same title in the Kegan Paul Library of Sexual Life (London: Kegan Paul, 2002). Citations below are from the 1877 edition.

16. Cooper, *A History of the Rod*, 8.

17. In later decades the scandalous nature of such allegations would often be couched in psychoanalytical terms. See Scott, *The History of Corporal Punishment*; and Van Yelyr, *The Whip and the Rod*.

18. Cooper, *A History of the Rod*, 214.

19. Ibid., 231-232.

20. Ibid., 234.

21. Ibid., 240.

22. Ibid., 242. On the complex politics of tsarist Russia's penal practices, see Schrader, *Languages of the Lash*. Not surprisingly, Russian promoters of reforming corporal punishment construed its prevalence as a poisonous legacy of the Tartars. See ibid., 150-151 and 175-182.

23. Cooper, *A History of the Rod*, 145-146.

24. Ibid., 14-15.

25. Newman, *Just and Painful*, 34.

26. Scarry, *The Body in Pain*; DelVecchio Good, et al., *Pain as Human Experience*; Käll, *Dimensions of Pain*.

27. Haenen, 'Eén keer met te veel op achter het stuur'.

28. http://chartsbin.com/view/eqq (last accessed 13 December 2013).

29. http://tarlton.law.utexas.edu/exhibits/ww_justice/ruiz_v_estelle.html (last accessed 26 November 2013). A Consent Decree (1981) issued as a compromise between the sides has been only partially fulfilled and continued litigation prompted Congressional intervention in the form of a Prison Litigation Reform Act (1996), which curbed inmates' capacity to challenge their conditions of incarceration in a law court.

30. Johnson and Toch, *The Pains of Imprisonment*; Bottoms and Light, *Problems of Long-Term Imprisonment*; Hensley, *Prison Sex*; Haney, *Reforming Punishment*; Cusac, *Cruel and Unusual*.

31. *Oxford English Dictionary*, s.v. 'Corporal'.

32. See Garland, *Peculiar Institution*, 206-230. In a grim development, a ban on exporting sodium thiopental, one of the drug cocktail's ingredients, from Europe to the US for execution purposes, several states introduced new drug combinations, which seem to extend physical suffering even further. See http://edition.cnn.com/2014/01/16/justice/ohio-dennis-mcguire-execution (last accessed 22 January 2014); and http://www.nytimes.com/2014/07/24/us/arizona-takes-nearly-2-hours-to-execute-inmate.html?hp&action=click&pgtype=Homepage&version=HpSum&module=first-column-region&region=top-news&WT.nav=top-news (last accessed 24 July 2014).

33. http://www.deathpenaltyinfo.org/methods-execution (last accessed 20 June 2013).

34. Geltner, *The Medieval Prison*.

35. *Codex Theodosianus*, 9.3.1: 'Ne poenis carceris perimetur, quod innocentibus miserum, noxiis non satis severum esse cognoscitur'.

36. Malynes, *Consuedo, vel, Lex Mercatoria*, 431.

37. Sère and Wettlaufer, *Shame between Punishment and Penance*.

38. Geertz, 'Thick Description'.

39. For an excellent illustration see Schrader, *Languages of the Lash*.

40. Westbrook, *A History of Ancient Near Eastern Law*, 74-75. And see the elegant articulation of this trope in Islamic descriptions of the afterlife by Asin y Palacios, *Islam and the Divine Comedy*, 96, n. 1.

41. Liancheng and Wenming, 'Society during the Three Dynasties', 170.

42. Fu, *Autocratic Tradition and Chinese Politics*, 109.

43. Hsiao, 'Legalism and Autocracy in Traditional China', 127-128.

44. Te Haar, 'Violence in Chinese Religious Culture'.

45. Hulsewé, *Remnants of Han Law*.

46. Miethe and Lu, *Punishment*, 124-128.

47. Van Gulik, *Crime and Punishment in Ancient China*.

48. Spence, *The Death of Woman Wang*, 120-138; Miethe and Lu, *Punishment*, 130-132 and 141-143. And see ibid., 141, n. 110, where the authors acknowledge the potentially vast gap between the legal abolition of corporal punishment and its ubiquitous practice.

49. Nineteenth-century picture albums produced in China and aimed at Western audiences contained images of local penal customs such as punishment by cangue or wooden pillory. Several of these albums, generically entitled 'Punishment and

Execution of Chinese Criminals', can be found in Harvard University Library's Olivia catalog, at nos. 130-132.

50. Lahiri, *Crime and Punishment in Ancient India*, 170.

51. Olivelle, *Manu's Code of Law*, 9.237 (202). Kane, *History of Dharmaśāstra*, vol. 2.1, 81 and n. 188, places dogs, together with cripples and caṇḍālas, on the same level as beings to be avoided, which explains the demeaning nature of being branded with the sign of a dog's paw.

52. Doongaji, *Crime and Punishment*, 148-187; Kharade, *Society in the Atharvaveda*, 56-58.

53. The earliest extant legal prescripts from this region, promulgated by Lipit-Ishtar (*c*. 1870 BCE-1860 BCE), make no mention of punishments other than monetary fines. See Roth, *Law Collections from Mesopotamia and Asia Minor*, 23-35.

54. George, *Cuneiform Royal Inscriptions*, 221-286.

55. Tetlow, *Women, Crime, and Punishment*, 1:199; Westbrook, *A History of Ancient Near Eastern Law*, 651.

56. Hoffner, *The Laws of the Hittites*, §95.

57. 'Laws of Hammurabi', in Roth, *Law Collections*, 71-142 at 121.

58. Westbrook, *A History of Ancient Near Eastern Law*, 553.

59. Tetlow, *Women, Crime, and Punishment,* 1:135 and 139. Despite its declared focus, the work demonstrates that the fluctuation of physical punishments ('severity') applies to women as well as men across the social strata.

60. Westbrook, *A History of Ancient Near Eastern Law*, 553-612. And see ibid., 906 and 966, respectively, for rare instances of corporal punishment in the Neo-Assyrian Period (10th-7th century BCE) and under the Chaldean Empire (late 7th-mid-6th century BCE).

61. See Kataja and Whiting, *Grants, Decrees and Gifts of the Neo-Assyrian Period*, 93 (fig. 16).

62. Westbrook, *A History of Ancient Near Eastern Law*, 131.

63. VerSteeg, *Law in Ancient Egypt*, 151-186.

64. Lorton, 'The Treatment of Criminals in Ancient Egypt'.

65. Westbrook, *A History of Ancient Near Eastern Law*, 342.

66. The veritable explosion of newly discovered documents from the ancient Near East is bound to alter this state of affairs.

67. Saunders, *Plato's Penal Code*.

68. Allen, *The World of Prometheus*.

69. Tetlow, *Women, Crime, and Punishment*, vol. 2.

70. Robinson, *Penal Practice and Penal Policy in Ancient Rome*. And see Tetlow, *Women, Crime, and Punishment* 2:138 and 144.

71. Suetonius, *The Lives of the Twelve Caesars*, 429-430.

72. Cascione, *Tresviri capitales*.

73. *Digesta Iustiniani Augusti*, 48.19.28.5: 'omnes, qui fustibus caedi prohibentur, eandem habere honoris reverentiam debet, quam decuriones habent'.

74. *The Letter of Tansar*, 33.

75. Ibid., 39-41.

76. Ibid., 42.

77. Ibid., 42-43.

78. Jullien, 'Peines et supplices dans les Actes des martyres persans et droit sassanide'.

79. *The Zend Avesta*, I, Farfard IV, 18-21 (58-72).

80. Law, *Religious Reflections on the Human Body*.

81. See Baker, *Plain Ugly*, 41-68.

82. The rich ambiguity of Cain's penal process and its aftermath are brilliantly explored in José Saramago's last novel, *Cain* (2009). Less ambiguous personal marks feature in other biblical texts, such as Ezekiel 9:4-5 and Revelation 14:1, where the righteous are marked on their foreheads.

83. Goldin, *Hebrew Criminal Law and Procedure*.

84. *Encyclopedia Judaica Online*, s.v. 'Flogging': http://www.jewishvirtuallibrary.org/jsource/judaica/ejud_0002_0007_0_06574.html (last accessed 15 June 2013).

85. See, for instance, *The Jewish Encyclopedia*, s.v. 'Corporal Punishment': http://www.jewishencyclopedia.com/articles/4672-corporal-punishment (last accessed 27 June 2013).

86. *Judean Antiquities* 4.8.21 and 23.

87. Jacob and Zemer, *Crime and Punishment in Jewish Law*.

88. Biale, *Power and Powerlessness in Jewish History*.

89. Cohn, 'Criminal Law Reform in Israel', 5.

90. Haj, *Disability in Antiquity*, 108.

91. Lange, *Justice, Punishment and the Medieval Muslim Imagination*, 77-79.

92. Averroēs, *The Distinguished Jurist's Primer*, 56.6.2.

93. Ibn Hajar al-'Asqālani, *Bulūgh al-maram*, 1064-1066.

94. Türkmenoglu, *Das Strafrecht des klassischen islamischen Rechts*, 91-118.

95. Lange and Fierro, 'Introduction'.

96. Lange, *Justice, Punishment and the Medieval Muslim Imagination*, 79-89.

97. On medieval etiologies of impairment see Metzler, *Disability in Medieval Europe*, 71-98.

98. Haj, *Disability in Antiquity*, 139-140; Richardson, *Difference and Disability*.

99. Richardson, *Difference and Disability*, 30. Lange, *Justice, Punishment and the Medieval Muslim Imagination*, 139-175.

100. Cited from Mediano, 'Justice, Crime and Punishment in 10th/16th-Century Morocco', in Lange and Fierro, *Public Violence in Islamic Societies*, 184.

101. Peters, *Crime and Punishment in Islamic Law*.

102. Frembgan, 'Honour, Shame, and Bodily Mutilation'.

103. Naipaul, *Among the Believers*; Kadri, *Heaven on Earth*, 211-236. The Sultan of Brunei recently announced that the country's religious law courts' jurisdiction will soon extend into the criminal sphere: http://www.afp.com/en/node/1130891 (last accessed 22 October 2013).

104. Kuefler, 'Castration and Eunuchism in the Middle Ages'; idem, *The Manly Eunuch*. And see Tracy, *Castration and Culture in the Middle Ages*, a collection that deftly illustrates the polyvalence of castration as an act perpetrated and perceived.

105. Goosmann, 'The Long-Haired Kings of the Franks'.

106. 'Penitential of St. Columbanus', in Bieler, *The Irish Penitentials*, 99 and 107, respectively.

107. 'The *Regula Coenobialis* of Columban', in McNeill and Gamer, *Medieval Handbooks of Penance*, 264-265.

108. Hillner, 'Monks and Children'.

109. 'Old Irish Table of Commutations', in McNeill and Gamer, *Medieval Handbooks of Penance*, 144.

110. De Vogüe, *Histoire littéraire du mouvement monastique dans l'Antiquité*, 1:94.

111. For a survey of this iconographical tradition see Piccat, 'Dalle raffigurazioni medievali a "The Passion"'.

112. *Acts of the Christian Martyrs*, Pionius 7 and Agape 5-6 (147 and 292, respectively).

113. Elishē, *History of Vardan and the Armenian War*, 175 and 232, respectively.

114. Upson-Saia, 'Resurrecting Deformity'. See also Bynum, 'Material Continuity, Personal Survival, and the Resurrection of the Body'.

115. Plöchl, *Geschichte des Kirchenrechts*. See Biller and Minnis, *Handling Sin*, for recent debates on audiences and practices.
116. Bieler, *The Irish Penitentials*, 153; McNeil and Gamer, *Medieval Handbooks of Penance*, 142, 144, 163, 231, 236, 238, 272, 289-290, 347, 355, and 389.
117. Parsons, 'The Way of the Rod'.
118. On the relations between Christian and Islamic imaginations of the afterlife see Asin y Palacios, *Islam and the Divine Comedy*.
119. Henderson, 'The Flagellant Movement'; Merback, 'Living Image of Pity'.
120. Merback, *The Thief, the Cross and the Wheel*, 126-157; Groebner, *Defaced*, 87-123. And see Edgerton, *Pictures and Punishment*; and Mills, *Suspended Animation*.
121. Greenblatt, 'Mutilation and Meaning', 223.
122. Falconer, *Crime and Community in Reformation Scotland*; Schilling, '"History of Crime" or "History of Sin"?'.
123. Pihlajamäki, 'Executor diviniarum et suarum legum'.
124. Classen, *The Medieval Chastity Belt*.
125. Yawn, 'The Bright Side of the Knife'.
126. Foucault, *Discipline and Punish*, 8.
127. Berman, *Law and Revolution*; Bellomo, *The Common Legal Past of Europe*.
128. Dean, *Crime in Medieval Europe*, 118-143.
129. Dean, *Crime and Justice in Late Medieval Italy*, 36-37, 48-49, and 198-199.
130. *Statuta populi et communis Florentiae*, Book III, XXVII (1:247).
131. Pollock and Maitland, *The History of English Law*, 2:452-253 and 458-462.
132. Patlagean, 'Byzance et le blason pénal du corps'.
133. Caviness, 'Giving "the Middle Ages" a Bad Name'.
134. Dean, *Crime and Justice in Late Medieval Italy*; but see Piasentini, '*Alla luce della luna*'.
135. Bellamy, *Crime and Public Order in England in the Later Middle Ages*.
136. Spierenburg, *The Spectacle of Suffering*.
137. Langbein, *Prosecuting Crime in the Renaissance*; Andrews, *Law, Magistracy and Crime in Old Regime Paris*; Jeanclos, *Les atteintes corporelles*.
138. Hibbert, *The Roots of Evil*, 408-409.
139. Ten Cate, '*Tot glorie der gerechtigheid*'.

140. Gonthier, *Le châtiment du crime au Moyen Age*, 140-146.
141. Ten Cate, 'Tot glorie der gerechtigheid', 81-83.
142. Veldhuizen, 'De ongetemde tong', 144-145; Ewan, 'Tongue, You Lied'.
143. Østergård, 'Denmark: A Big Small State', 63-64.
144. Gates and Marafioti, 'Introduction', 8; O'Gorman, 'Mutilation and Spectacle'.
145. Herrin, 'Blinding in Byzantium'; Tougher, *The Eunuch in Byzantine History and Society*; idem, *Eunuchs in Antiquity and Beyond*. On the stigmas attendant upon blindness see Wheatley, *Stumbling Blocks Before the Blind*.
146. Skinner, 'The Gendered Nose and its Lack'.
147. Groebner, *Defaced*, 32 and 84-86.
148. Veldhuizen, 'De ongetemde tong', 149-150.
149. Origo, 'The Domestic Enemy', 341 and n. 97; Brucker, *The Society of Renaissance Florence*, 222-228; Orme, *Medieval Children*, 84-85 and 154-157.
150. Groebner, *Defaced*, 42.
151. Beccaria, *On Crimes and Punishments*; Bentham, *The Rationale of Punishment*. The latter is a posthumous work based on the French reworking of Bentham's original in Dumont, *Théorie des peines et des récompenses*.
152. Gibson, 'Global Perspectives on the Birth of the Prison'. An updated bibliography of prison history is: www.falk-bretschneider.eu/biblio/biblio-index.htm (last accessed 11 November 2013).
153. Foucault, *Discipline and Punish*; Rothman, *The Discovery of the Asylum*; Ignatieff, *A Just Measure of Pain*; Melosi and Pavarini, *The Prison and the Factory*; Shoemaker, 'The Problem of Pain in Punishment'.
154. Bentham, *The Rationale of Punishment*, II, 1, §1 (82).
155. Jefferson, *Writings*, 350-356.
156. See De Vito and Lichtenstein, 'Writing a History of Convict Labour'.
157. Gibson, 'Cesare Lombroso, Prison Science, and Penal Policy', 42.
158. Schaaff, 'De lijfstraf als disciplinaire straf in de wet van 14 April 1886'.
159. Weisser, *Crime and Punishment in Early Modern Europe*.
160. Lanjuinais, *La Bastonnade et la Flagellation*, i.
161. Bentley, *English Criminal Justice in the Nineteenth Century*, 12-13.
162. Salt, *The Flogging Craze*, 24-25.

163. Van Yelyr, *The Whip and the Rod*, vii (italics original).

164. Benton, *Law and Colonial Cultures*; Peters, *Crime and Punishment in Islamic Law*.

165. Ávalos, 'An Overview of the Legal System of the Aztec Empire', 267-268.

166. Izquierdo, 'El Derecho Penal entre los Antiguos Mayas', 236.

167. Sayre, *Les Sauvages Américains*, 248-321.

168. Newell, *Crime and Justice among the Iroquois Nations*, 85-86.

169. Lévi-Strauss, *Tristes tropiques*, 388. And see Diamond, *The World Until Yesterday*, 79-97.

170. Newell, *Crime and Justice among the Iroquois*, 69, 72, and 83-85.

171. Miethe and Lu, *Punishment*, 91-92 and 96.

172. McNair, *Criminal Injustice*, 143-165, which also documents some instances of penal castration for sexual offenders.

173. Moore, *American Negro Slavery and Abolition*, 114-116; Campbell, *Crime and Punishment in African American History*, 87-112.

174. Ayers, *Vengeance and Justice*.

175. MacLachlan, *Criminal Justice in Eighteenth-Century Mexico*, 81.

176. Barreneche, *Crime and the Administration of Justice in Buenos Aires*, 73.

177. Holloway, *Policing Rio de Janeiro*, 60.

178. Ketting, *Leven, werk en rebellie aan boord van Oost-Indiëvaarders*, 269-290; Van Gelder, *Naporra's omweg*, 276-281.

179. Van Yelyr, *The Whip and the Rod*, 98-102; Blainey, *A Shorter History of Australia*, 220.

180. Salt, *The Flogging Craze*, 20-21; Banerjee, *The Wicked City*, 365-397.

181. Lyons, *The History of Punishment*, 90-93.

182. Scott, *The History of Corporal Punishment*, 184.

183. Gard, *The End of the Rod*.

184. Scott, *The History of Corporal Punishment*, 186.

185. Spalding, 'Florida's 1997 Chemical Castration Law'.

186. Ellison and Sherkat, 'Conservative Protestantism and Support for Corporal Punishment'; Straus, *Beating the Devil Out of Them*.

187. http://www.corpun.com/rules.htm (last accessed 20 January 2014).

188. Gelles, *The Violent Home*.

189. Gibson, *The English Vice*, 64.

190. See Pinker, *The Better Angels of Our Nature*, 435-441, who also acknowledges the methodological difficulties of assessing parents' attitudes toward spanking.

191. http://endcorporalpunishment.org/pages/frame.html (last accessed 20 January 2014).

192. Montagu, *Learning Non-Aggression*.

193. Parsons, 'The Way of the Rod'.

194. McCord, *Coercion and Punishment in Long-Term Perspectives*; Afifi, et al., 'Physical Punishment and Mental Disorders'.

195. Pearl and Pearl, *To Train Up a Child*. The Pearls' book has gone through eight reprints, two editions, two translations (into German and Chinese), and has reportedly sold more than 550,000 copies.

196. US Congress Committee on Education and Labor, Subcommittee on Healthy Families and Communities, 'Corporal Punishment in Schools and its Effect on Academic Success' (2010): http://www.gpo.gov/fdsys/pkg/CHRG-111hhrg55850/html/CHRG-111hhrg55850.htm (last accessed 25 July 2013).

197. Newman, *Just and Painful*; Moskos, *In Defense of Flogging*.

198. Lyons, *The History of Punishment*, 100-101.

199. On the diverse profiles of shaming and degradation in the modern West see Whitman, *Harsh Justice*.

200. Pinker, *The Better Angels of Our Nature*, 133. Pinker, a US-based academic and acclaimed public intellectual, is surely being ironic with respect to capital punishment in his own backyard. And see also n. 205 below.

201. Garland 'The Problem of the Body in Modern State Punishment'.

202. Terry and Urla, 'Introduction'; Turner, *The Body and Society*.

203. Siebers, *Disability Aesthetics*, is a compelling articulation of this argument.

204. http://www.liveleak.com/view?i=3c9_1304013159 (last accessed 28 November 2013). The campaign to abolish corporal punishment worldwide maintains http://www.corpun.com/vids.htm.

205. Nor is it apparently expedient to be reminded that Malaysia, like the US, practices capital punishment. Between 2007 and 2012 Malaysia (population 29.5 million) sentenced 324 people to death and executed two of them. During the same period, the US (population 316 million) issued 504 death sentences and carried out 220: http://www.amnesty.org.uk/news_details.asp?NewsID=20725 (last accessed 10 July 2013).

206. Geltner, 'History of Corporal Punishment'.

List of Illustrations

Works Cited

Afifi, Tracie O., et al., 'Physical Punishment and Mental Disorders: Results from a Nationally Representative US Sample', *Pediatrics*, 130 (2012), 1-8.

Allen, Danielle S., *The World of Prometheus: The Politics of Punishing in Democratic Athens* (Princeton: Princeton University Press, 2000).

Andrews, Richard Mowery, *Law, Magistracy and Crime in Old Regime Paris, 1735-1789* (New York: Cambridge University Press, 1994).

Asin y Palacios, Miguel, *Islam and the Divine Comedy*, ed. and trans. Harold Sunderland (London: Cass, 1968).

Ávalos, Francisco, 'An Overview of the Legal System of the Aztec Empire', *Law Library Journal*, 86 (1994), 259-276.

Averroës, *The Distinguished Jurist's Primer: A Translation of Bidāyat al-mujtahid*, trans. Imram Ahsan, 2 vols. (Reading, UK: Garnet, 1994-1996).

Ayers, Edward L., *Vengeance and Justice: Crime and Punishment in the 19th-Century South* (New York and Oxford: Oxford University Press, 1984).

Baker, Naomi, *Plain Ugly: The Unattractive Body in Early Modern Culture* (Manchester: Manchester University Press, 2010).

Banerjee, Sumanta, *The Wicked City: Crime and Punishment in Colonial Calcutta* (New Delhi: Orient BlackSwan, 2009).

Barney, Charles Norton, *Circumcision and Flagellation among the Filipinos* (Carlisle, PA: Association of Military Surgeons, 1903).

Barreneche, Osvaldo, *Crime and the Administration of Justice in Buenos Aires, 1785-1853* (Lincoln, NB: University of Nebraska Press, 2006).

Beccaria, Cesare, *On Crimes and Punishments, and Other Writings*, ed. Richard Bellamy; trans. Richard Davies (Cambridge, UK: Cambridge University Press, 1995).

Bellamy, John G., *Crime and Public Order in England in the Later Middle Ages* (London: Routledge and Kegan Paul, 1973).

Bellomo, Manlio, *The Common Legal Past of Europe, 1000-1800*, trans. Lydia G. Cochrane (Washington, D.C.: Catholic University of America Press, 1995).

Bentham, Jeremy, *The Rationale of Punishment* (London: Robert Heward, 1830).

Bentley, David, *English Criminal Justice in the Nineteenth Century* (London: Hambledon Press, 1998).

Benton, Lauren A., *Law and Colonial Cultures: Legal Regimes in World History, 1400-1900* (Cambridge, UK: Cambridge University Press, 2002).

Berman, Harold J., *Law and Revolution: The Formation of the Western Legal Tradition* (Cambridge, MA: Harvard University Press, 1983).

Biale, David, *Power and Powerlessness in Jewish History* (New York: Schocken Books, 1987).

Bieler, Ludwig (ed.), *The Irish Penitentials*, Scriptores Latini Hiberniae 5 (Dublin: Dublin Institute for Advanced Studies, 1963).

Biller, Peter, and A.J. Minnis (eds.), *Handling Sin: Confession in the Middle Ages* (Woodbridge, Suffolk and Rochester, NY: York Medieval Press, 1998).

Blainey, Geoffrey, *A Shorter History of Australia*, rev. ed. (Sydney: Random House, 2000).

Boilleau, Jacques, *History of Flagellation among Different Nations* (London: [s.n.], 1888).

Bottoms, Anthony E., and Roy Light (eds.), *Problems of Long-Term Imprisonment* (Aldershot, UK: Gower, 1987).

Brucker, Gene (ed. and trans.), *The Society of Renaissance Florence: A Documentary Study* (New York: Harper Torchbooks, 1971).

Bussler. E., *Die Prügelstrafe* (Eberswalde: Langewiesche & Thilo, 1906).

Bynum, Caroline Walker, 'Material Continuity, Personal Survival, and the Resurrection of the Body: A Scholastic Discussion and Its Medieval and Modern Contexts', *History of Religions*, 30 (1990), 51-85.

Cabanès, Augustin, *Flagellation in France from a Medical and Historical Standpoint* (Paris: Charles Carrington, 1898).

Campbell, James, *Crime and Punishment in African American History* (New York: Palgrave Macmillan, 2013).

Cascione, Cosimo, *Tresviri capitales. Storia di una magistratura minore* (Naples: Editoriale Scientifica, 1999).

Caviness, Madeline, 'Giving "the Middle Ages" a Bad Name: Blood Punishments in the *Sachsenspiegel* and Town Lawbooks', *Studies in Iconography*, 34 (2013), 175-235.

Classen, Albercht, *The Medieval Chastity Belt: A Myth-Making Process* (Houndmills, Basingstoke: Palgrave Macmillan, 2008).

Clutton-Brock, T.H., and G.A. Parker, 'Punishment in Animal Societies', *Nature*, 373 (1995), 209-216.

Codex Theodosianus, ed. Theodor Mommsen and Paul Krueger, 2 vols. in 3 (Hildesheim: Weidmann, 1990 [orig. publ. 1905]).

Cohn, Haim, 'Criminal Law Reform in Israel', *The American University Law Review*, 11 (1962), 1-20.

Cooper, William M. [James Glass Bertram], *Flagellation and the Flagellants: A History of the Rod in All Countries from the Earliest Periods to the Present Time* (London: William Reeves, 1840).

Cusac, Anne-Marie, *Cruel and Unusual: The Culture of Punishment in America* (New Haven and London: Yale University Press, 2009).

Dean, Trevor, *Crime in Medieval Europe, 1200-1550* (London: Longman, 2001).

Dean, Trevor, *Crime and Justice in Late Medieval Italy* (Cambridge, UK: Cambridge University Press, 2007).

DelVecchio Good, Mary-Jo, et al. (eds.), *Pain as Human Experience: An Anthropological Perspective* (Berkeley: University of California Press, 1992).

De Vito, Christian G., and Alex Lichtenstein, 'Writing a History of Convict Labour', *International Review of Social History*, 58 (2013), 285-325.

Diamond, Jared, *The World Until Yesterday: What Can We Learn from Traditional Societies* (New York: Viking, 2012).

Digesta Iustiniani Augusti, ed. Theodor Mommsen and Paul Krueger, 2 vols. (Berlin: Weidmann, 1870).

Doongaji, Damayanti, *Crime and Punishment in Ancient Hindu Society* (Jawahar Nagar: Ajanta, 1986).

Douglas, Mary, *Purity and Danger* (London and New York: Routledge, 2002 [orig. publ. 1966]).

Dumont, Étienne, *Théorie des peines et des récompenses* (London: Vogel & Schulze, 1811).

Durkheim, Émile, 'Two Laws of Penal Evolution', in *The Radical Sociology of Durkheim and Mauss*, ed. Mike Gane (London and New York: Routledge, 1992), 21-49.

Edgerton, Samuel Y., *Pictures and Punishment: Art and Criminal Prosecution during the Florentine Renaissance* (Ithaca: Cornell University Press, 1985).

Elias, Norbert, *The Civilizing Process*, trans. Edmund Jephcott (Oxford: Basil Blackwell, 1994 [orig. publ. 1939]).

Elishē, *History of Vardan and the Armenian War*, trans. Robert W. Thomson (Cambridge, MA, and London: Harvard University Press, 1982).

Ellison, Christopher G., and Darren E. Sherkat, 'Conservative Protestantism and Support for Corporal Punishment', *American Sociological Review*, 58 (1993), 131-144.

Ewan, Elizabeth, '"Tongue, You Lied". The Role of the Tongue in Rituals of Public Penance in Late Medieval Scotland', in *The Hands of the Tongue: Essays on Deviant Speech*, ed. Edwin D. Craun (Kalamazoo, MI: Medieval institute Publications, 2007), 115-136.

Falconer, J.R.D., *Crime and Community in Reformation Scotland: Negotiating Power in a Burgh Society* (London: Pickering & Chatto, 2013).

Filkins, Dexter, 'The Thin Red Line', *The New Yorker*, 13 May 2013.

Foucault, Michel, *Discipline and Punish: The Birth of the Prison*, trans. Alan Sheridan (London: Penguin Books, 1991).

Frembgen, Jürgen Wasim, 'Honour, Shame, and Bodily Mutilation: Cutting off the Nose among Tribal Societies in Pakistan', *Journal of the Royal Asiatic Society of Great Britain & Ireland*, 16 (2006), 243-260.

Fu, Zhengyuan, *Autocratic Tradition and Chinese Politics* (Cambridge, UK: Cambridge University Press, 1993).

Gard, Raymond L., *The End of the Rod: A History of the Abolition of Corporal Punishment in the Courts of England and Wales* (Boca Raton: BrownWalker Press, 2009).

Garland, David 'The Problem of the Body in Modern State Punishment', *Social Research*, 78 (2011), 767-798.

Garland, David, *Peculiar Institution: America's Death Penalty in an Age of Abolition* (Cambridge, MA: Belknap Press, 2010).

Gates, Jay Paul, and Nicole Marafioti, 'Introduction', in *Capital and Corporal Punishment in Anglo-Saxon England*, ed. Jay Paul Gates and Nicole Marafioti (London: Boydell, 2014), 1-16.

Geertz, Clifford, 'Thick Description: Toward an Interpretative Theory of Culture', in *The Interpretation of Cultures: Selected Essays* (New York: Basic Books, 1973), 3-30.

Gelder, Roelof van, *Naporra's omweg. Het leven van een VOC-matroos (1731-1793)* (Amsterdam and Antwerp: Atlas, 2003).

Gelles, Richard J., *The Violent Home*, rev. ed. (Newbury Park, CA: Sage, 1987).

Geltner, G., *The Medieval Prison: A Social History* (Princeton: Princeton University Press, 2008).

Geltner, G., 'History of Corporal Punishment', in *Encyclopedia of Criminology and Criminal Justice*, gen. ed. Gerben Bruinsma and David Weisburd, 10 vols. [successively numbered] (New York: Springer, 2014), 2106-2115.

George, Andrew (ed.), *Cuneiform Royal Inscriptions and Related Texts in the Schøyen Collection,* Cornell University Studies in Assyriology and Sumerology 17, Manuscripts in the Schøyen Collection, Cuneiform Texts VI (Bethesda, MD: CDL Press, 2011).

Gibson, Ian, *The English Vice: Beating, Sex and Shame in Victorian England and After* (London: Duckworth, 1978).

Gibson, Mary, 'Global Perspectives on the Birth of the Prison', *American Historical Review*, 116 (2011), 1040-1063.

Gibson, Mary, 'Cesare Lombroso, Prison Science, and Penal Policy', in *The Cesare Lombroso Handbook*, ed. Paul Knepper and Jørgen Ystehede (Abingdon, UK and New York: Routledge, 2013), 30-46.

Girgen, Jen, 'The Historical and Contemporary Prosecution of Animals', *Animal Law*, 9 (2003), 97-134.

Glucklich, Ariel, 'The Royal Scepter (*Danda*) as Legal and Sacred Symbol', *History of Religions*, 28 (1988), 97-122.

Goldin, Hyman E., *Hebrew Criminal Law and Procedure. Mishnah: Sanhedrin – Makkot* (New York: Twayne, 1952).

Gonthier, Nicole, *Le châtiment du crime au Moyen Age: XIIe-XVIe siècles* (Rennes: Presses Universitaires de Rennes, 1998).

Goosmann, Erik, 'The Long-Haired Kings of the Franks: "Like So Many Samsons?"', *Early Medieval Europe*, 20 (2013), 233-259.

Greenblatt, Stephen, 'Mutilation and Meaning', in *The Body in Parts: Fantasies of Corporeality in Early Modern Europe*, ed. David Hillmans and Carla Mazzio (New York and London: Routledge, 1997), 221-241.

Groebner, Valentin, *Defaced: The Visual Culture of Violence in the Late Middle Ages*, trans. Pamela Selwyn (New York: Zone Books, 2004).

Guénolé, Pierre, *L'étrange passion: la flagellation dans les mœurs d'aujourd'hui* (Paris: Office Central de Librairie, 1904).

Gulik, Robert Hans van, *Crime and Punishment in Ancient China: T'ang-Yin-Pi-Shih*, 2nd edn. (Bangkok: Orchid Press, 2007).

Haenen, Marcel, 'Eén keer met te veel op achter het stuur, en meteen een alcohol-slot', *NRC Handelsblad*, 16 July 2014.

Haj, Fareed, *Disability in Antiquity* (New York: Philosophical Library, 1970).

Haney, Craig, *Reforming Punishment: Psychological Limits to the Pains of Imprisonment* (Washington, D.C.: American Psychological Association, 2006).

Henderson, John, 'The Flagellant Movement and Flagellant Confraternities in Central Italy, 1260-1400', *Studies in Church History*, 15 (1978), 147-160.

Hensley, Christopher (ed.), *Prison Sex: Practice and Policy* (Boulder, CO: Lynne Rienner, 2002).

Herrin, Judith, 'Blinding in Byzantium', in *Polypleuros nous: Miscellanea für Peter Schreiner zu seinem 60. Geburtstag*, ed. Cordula Scholz and Georgios Makris (Munich: Sur, 2000), 56-68.

Hibbert, Christopher, *The Roots of Evil: A Social History of Crime and Punishment* (Boston and Toronto: Little, Brown, and Company, 1963).

Hillner, Julia, 'Monks and Children: Corporal Punishment in Late Antiquity', *European Review of History-Revue européenne d'histoire*, 16 (2009), 773-791.

Hoffner, Harry A., *The Laws of the Hittites: A Critical Edition* (Leiden: Brill, 1997).

Holloway, Thomas H., *Policing Rio de Janeiro: Repression and Resistance in a 19th-Century City* (Stanford, CA: Stanford University Press, 1993).

Hsiao, Kung-chuan, 'Legalism and Autocracy in Traditional China', in *Shang Yang's Reforms and State Control in China*, ed. Li Yu-ning (White Plains, NY: M.E. Sharpe, 1977), 125-143.

Hulsewé, A.F.P., *Remnants of Han Law* (Leiden: Brill, 1955).

Ibn Hajar al-ʿAsqalānī, Ahmad ibn ʿAli, *Bulūgh al-maram min adilat al-ahkāam=Attainment of the Objective According to Evidence of the Ordinances* (Riyadh: Dār al-Salām, 1996).

Ignatieff, Michael, *A Just Measure of Pain: The Penitentiary in the Industrial Revolution, 1750-1850* (New York: Pantheon Books, 1978).

Izquierdo, Ana Luisa, 'El Derecho Penal entre los Antiguos Mayas', *Estudios de Cultura Maya*, 11 (1978), 215-247.

Jacob, Walter, and Moshe Zemer (eds.), *Crime and Punishment in Jewish Law: Essays and Responsa* (New York: Berghahan, 1999).

Jeanclos, Yves (ed.), *Les atteintes corporelles causes à la victime et imposes au condamné en France du XVIe siècle à nos jours* (Strasbourg: Université Robert Schuman, Faculté de droit, de sciences politiques et de gestion, 1999).

Jefferson, Thomas, *Writings*, ed. Merrill D. Peterson (New York: Viking, 1984).

Johnson, Robert, and Hans Toch (eds.), *The Pains of Imprisonment* (Beverly Hills, CA: Sage, 1982).

Josephus, Flavius, *Judean Antiquities 1-4*, trans. Louis H. Feldman (Leiden: Brill, 2000).

Jullien, Christelle, 'Peines et supplices dans les Actes des martyres persans et droit sassanide: nouvelles prospections', *Studia Iranica*, 33 (2004), 243-269.

Kadri, Sadakat, *Heaven on Earth* (New York: Farrar, Straus and Giroux, 2012).

Käll, Lisa Folkmarson (ed.), *Dimensions of Pain: Humanities and Social Science Perspectives* (Abingdon, UK, and New York: Routledge, 2013).

Kane, P.V., *History of Dharmaśāstra* (Poona: Bhandarkar Oriental Research Institute, 1941).

Kataja, L., and R. Whiting (eds.), *Grants, Decrees and Gifts of the Neo-Assyrian Period*, State Archives of Assyria 12 (Helsinki: Helsinki University Press, 1995).

Ketting, H., *Leven, werk en rebellie aan boord van Oost-Indiëvaarders (1595-1650)* (Amsterdam: Askant, 2002).

Kharade, B.S., *Society in the Atharvaveda* (New Delhi: D.K. Printworld, 1997).

Kuefler, Mathew S., 'Castration and Eunuchism in the Middle Ages', in *The Handbook of Medieval Sexuality*, ed. Vern L. Bullough and James A. Brundage (New York: Garland Publishing, 1996), 279-306.

Kuefler, Mathew S., *The Manly Eunuch: Masculinity, Gender Ambiguity, and Christian Ideology in Late Antiquity* (Chicago: The University of Chicago Press, 2001).

Lahiri, Tārāpada, *Crime and Punishment in Ancient India* (New Delhi: Radiant Publishers, 1986).

Langbein, John H., *Prosecuting Crime in the Renaissance: England, Germany, France* (Cambridge, MA: Harvard University Press, 1974).

Lange, Christian, *Justice, Punishment and the Medieval Muslim Imagination* (Cambridge, UK: Cambridge University Press, 2008).

Lange, Christian, and Maribel Fierro, 'Introduction', in *Public Violence in Islamic Societies*, ed. Christian Lange and Maribel Fierro (Edinburgh: Edinburgh University Press, 2009), 1-23.

Lanjuinais, Jean-Denis, *La bastonnade et la flagellation pénales considérées chez les peuples anciens et chez les modernes* (Paris: Baudouin, 1825).

Law, Jane Marie (ed.), *Religious Reflections on the Human Body* (Bloomington and Indianapolis: Indiana University Press, 1995).

Lévi-Strauss, Claude, *Tristes tropiques*, trans. John and Doreen Weightman (London: Penguin Books, 1992 [orig. publ. 1955]).

Liancheng, Lu, and Yan Wenming, 'Society during the Three Dynasties', in Kwang-chih Chang, et al., *The Formation of Chinese Civilization. An Archaeological Perspective*, ed. Sarah Allan (New Haven and London: Yale University Press, 2005), 141-201.

Lorton, David, 'The Treatment of Criminals in Ancient Egypt', *Journal of the Economic and Social History of the Orient*, 20 (1976), 2-64.

Lyons, Lewis, *The History of Punishment* (London: Amber Books, 2003).

MacLachlan, Colin M., *Criminal Justice in Eighteenth-Century Mexico: A Study of the Tribunal of the Acordada* (Berkeley: The University of California Press, 1974).

Malynes, Gerard de, *Consuedo, vel, Lex Mercatoria* (London: Adam Islip, 1622).

Mariottini Spagnoli, Maria, 'The Symbolic Meaning of the Club in the Iconography of the Kuṣāṇa Kings', *East and West*, 17 (1967), 248-267.

McCord, Joan (ed.), *Coercion and Punishment in Long-Term Perspectives* (New York: Cambridge University Press, 1995).

McNair, Glenn, *Criminal Injustice: Slaves and Free Blacks in Georgia's Criminal Justice System* (Charlottesville, VA: University of Virginia Press, 2009).

McNeill, John, and Helena M. Gamer (eds. and trans.), *Medieval Handbooks of Penance* (New York: Columbia University Press, 1990 [orig. publ. 1938]).

Melosi, Dario, and Massimo Pavarini, *The Prison and the Factory: Origins of the Penitentiary System*, trans. Glynis Cousin (Totowa, NJ: Barnes and Noble Books, 1981).

Merback, Mitchell B., *The Thief, the Cross and the Wheel: Pain and the Spectacle of Punishment in Medieval and Renaissance Europe* (London: Reaktion Books, 1999).

Merback, Mitchell B., 'Living Image of Pity: Mimetic Violence, Peace-Making and Salvific Spectacle in the Flagellant Processions of the Later Middle Ages', in *Images of Medieval Sanctity: Essays in Honour of Gary Dickson*, ed. Debra Higgs Strickland (Leiden: Brill, 2007), 135-184.

Metzler, Irina, *Disability in Medieval Europe: Thinking about Physical Impairment during the High Middle Ages*, c. 1100-1400 (London: Routledge, 2006).

Miethe, Terance D., and Hong Lu, *Punishment: A Comparative Historical Perspective* (Cambridge, UK: Cambridge University Press, 2005).

Mills, Robert, *Suspended Animation: Pain, Pleasure, and Punishment in Medieval Culture* (London: Reaktion Books, 2005).

Montagu, Ashley (ed.), *Learning Non-Aggression: The Experience of Non-Literate Societies* (New York: Oxford University Press, 1978).

Moore, Wilbert Ellis, *American Negro Slavery and Abolition: A Sociological Study* (New York: The Third Press, 1971).

Moskos, Peter, *In Defense of Flogging* (New York: Basic Books, 2011).

Musurillo, Herbert (ed. and trans.), *Acts of the Christian Martyrs* (Oxford: Clarendon Press, 1972).

Naipaul, V.S., *Among the Believers: An Islamic Journey* (New York: Vintage Books, 1982).

Newell, William B., *Crime and Justice among the Iroquois Nations* (Montreal: Caughnawaga Historical Society, 1965).

Newman, Graeme, *Just and Painful. A Case for the Corporal Punishment of Criminals* (London: Macmillan, 1983).

O'Gorman, Dan, 'Mutilation and Spectacle in Anglo-Saxon Legislation', in *Capital and Corporal Punishment in Anglo-Saxon England*, ed. Jay Paul Gates and Nicole Marafioti (London: Boydell, 2014), 149-164.

Olivelle, Patrick, *Manu's Code of Law: A Critical Edition and Translation of the Mānava-Dharmaśāstra* (Oxford: Oxford University Press, 2005).

Origo, Iris, 'The Domestic Enemy: The Easter Slaves in Tuscany in the Fourteenth and Fifteenth Centuries', *Speculum*, 30 (1955), 321-366.

Orme, Nicholas, *Medieval Children* (New Haven: Yale University Press, 2001).

Østergård, Uffe, 'Denmark: A Big Small State: The Peasant Roots of Danish Modernity', in *National Identity and the Varieties of Capitalism: The Danish Experience*, ed. John Campbell, John A. Hall, and Ove K. Pedersen (Kingston, Ontario: McGill-Queen's University Press, 2006), 51-98.

Parsons, Ben, 'The Way of the Rod: The Functions of Beating in Medieval Pedagogy', *Modern Philology*, 113 (2015) [forthcoming].

Pape, H.M.M., *Ueber die Wiedereinführung der Prügelstrafe und die Züchtigung des Gesindes* (Insterburg: Wilhelmi, 1853).

Patlagean, Evelyne, 'Byzance et le blason pénal du corps', in *Du châtiment dans la cité. Supplices corporels et peine de mort dans le monde antique* (Rome: École française de Rome, 1984), 405-426.

Pearl, Michael and Debi Pearl, *To Train Up a Child* (Pleasantville, TN: NGJ Ministries, 1994).

Peters, Rudolph, *Crime and Punishment in Islamic Law: Theory and Practice from the Sixteenth to the Twenty-First Century* (Cambridge, UK: Cambridge University Press, 2005).

Piasentini, Stefano, *'Alla luce della luna': I furti a Venezia (1270-1403)* (Venice: Il Cardo, 1992).

Piccat, Marco, 'Dalle raffigurazioni medievali a "The Passion": l'invenzione degli "ebrei flagellanti"', *Mitteilungen des Kunsthistorischen Institutes in Florenz*, 49 (2005), 269-288.

Pihlajamäki, Heikki, 'Executor diviniarum et suarum legum: Criminal law and the Lutheran Reformation', in *Lutheran Reformation and the Law*, ed. V. Mäkinen (Leiden: Brill, 2006), 171-204.

Pinker, Steven, *The Better Angels of Our Nature: Why Violence has Declined* (New York: Viking, 2011).

Plöchl, Willibald M., *Geschichte des Kirchenrechts II: Das Kirchenrecht der abendländischen Christenheit 1055-1517* (Vienna: Herold, 1955).

Pollock, Frederick, and William Maitland, *The History of English Law before the Time of Edward I*, 2 vols. (Cambridge, UK: Cambridge University Press, 1952).

Resnik, Judith, and Dennis E. Curtis, 'Representing Justice: From Renaissance Iconography to Twenty-First-Century Courthouses', *Proceedings of the American Philosophical Society*, 151 (2007), 139-183.

Richardson, Kristina L., *Difference and Disability in the Medieval Islamic World: Blighted Bodies* (Edinburgh: Edinburgh University Press, 2012).

Robinson, O. F., *Penal Practice and Penal Policy in Ancient Rome* (New York: Routledge, 2007).

Roth, Martha T., *Law Collections from Mesopotamia and Asia Minor* (Atlanta: Scolars Press, 1995).

Rothman, David J., *The Discovery of the Asylum: Social Order and Disorder in the New Republic* (Boston: Little, Brown, 1971).

Salt, Henry S., *The Flogging Craze: A Statement of the Case Against Corporal Punishment* (London: George Allen & Unwin, 1916).

Saunders, Trevor J., *Plato's Penal Code: Tradition, Controversy, and Reform in Greek Penology* (Oxford: Clarendon Press, 1991).

Sayre, Gordon M., *Les Sauvages Américains: Representations of Native Americans in French and English Colonial Literature* (Chapel Hill, NC, and London: The University of North Carolina Press, 1997).

Scarry, Elaine, *The Body in Pain: The Making and Unmaking of the World* (New York: Oxford University Press, 1985).

Schaaff, Johannes Adam, 'De lijfstraf als disciplinaire straf in de wet van 14 April 1886 (Stbl. No. 62), tot vaststelling der beginselen van het gevangeniswezen' (PhD dissertation, University of Groningen, 1886).

Schilling, Heinz, '"History of Crime" or "History of Sin"? Reflections on the Social History of Early Modern Church Discipline', in *Politics and Society in Reformation Europe*, ed. E.I. Kouri and Tom Scott (London: Macmillan, 1987), 289-310.

Schor, Naomi, 'This Essentialism Which is Not One: Coming to Grips with Irigaray', in *The Essential Difference*, ed. Naomi Schor and Elizabeth Weed (Bloomington and Indianapolis: Indiana University Press, 1994), 40-62.

Schrader, Abby M., *Languages of the Lash: Corporal Punishment and Identity in Imperial Russia* (DeKalb, IL: Northern Illinois University Press, 2002).

Scott, George Ryley, *The History of Corporal Punishment* (London: Senate, 1996 [orig. publ. 1938]).

Sère, Bénédicte, and Jörg Wettlaufer (eds.), *Shame between Punishment and Penance*, Micrologus Library 111 (Florence: SISMEL, 2013).

Shoemaker, Karl, 'The Problem of Pain in Punishment: Historical Perspectives', in *Pain, Death, and the Law*, ed. Austin Sarat (Ann Arbor, MI: The University of Michigan Press, 2001), 15-41.

Siebers, Tobias, *Disability Aesthetics* (Ann Arbor, MI: The University of Michigan Press, 2010).

Skinner, Patricia, 'The Gendered Nose and its Lack', *Journal of Women's History*, 26 (2014), 45-67.

Smith, Philip, *Punishment and Culture* (Chicago: Chicago University Press, 2008).

Spalding, Larry Helm, 'Florida's 1997 Chemical Castration Law: A Return to the Dark Ages', *Florida State University Law Review*, 25 (1998), 117-139.

Spence, Jonathan D., *The Death of Woman Wang* (London: Weidenfeld and Nicolson, 1978).

Sperati, G., 'Amputation of the Nose Throughout History', *Acta Otorhinolaryngologica Italica*, 29 (2009), 44-50.

Spierenburg, Pieter C., *The Spectacle of Suffering* (Cambridge, UK: Cambridge University Press, 1984).

Spierenburg, Pieter C., *Violence and Punishment: Civilizing the Body through Time* (Cambridge, UK and Malden, MA: Polity, 2013).

Statuta populi et communis Florentiae...anno salutis MCCCCXV, 3 vols. (Freiburg: Michael Kluch, 1778-1783).

Straus, Murray A., with Denise A. Donnelly, *Beating the Devil Out of Them: Corporal Punishment in American Families* (New York: Lexington Books, 1994).

Suetonius, *The Lives of the Twelve Caesars*, trans. Alexander Thomson (Philadelphia: Gebbie & Co., 1889).

Te Haar, Barend J., 'Violence in Chinese Religious Culture', in *The Blackwell Companion to Religion and Violence*, ed. Andrew R. Murphy (Chichester, West Sussex, and Malden, MA: Wiley-Blackwell, 2011), 249-262.

Ten Cate, C.L., *'Tot glorie der gerechtigheid.' De geschiedenis van het brandmerken als lijfstraf in Nederland* (Amsterdam: Wetenschappelijke Uitgeverij, 1975).

Terry, Jennifer, and Jacqueline Urla, 'Introduction: Mapping Embodied Deviance', in *Deviant Bodies*, ed. Jennifer Terry and Jacqueline Urla (Bloomington and Indianapolis: Indiana University Press, 1995), 1-18.

Tetlow, Elisabeth Meier, *Women, Crime, and Punishment in Ancient Law and Society*, 2 vols. (New York and London: Continuum, 2004-2005).

The Book of a Thousand Judgements (*A Sasanian Law-Book*), ed. and trans. [to Russian] Anahit Perikhanian, English translation by Nin Garsoïan (Costa Mesa, CA, and New York: Mazda Publishers, 1980).

The Letter of Tansar, trans. M. Boyce (Rome: Istituto Italiano per il Medio ed Estremo Oriente, 1968).

The Zend Avesta, Part I, trans. James Darmesteter, Sacred Books of the East, 4 (Oxford: Clarendon Press, 1880).

Tougher, Shaun (ed.), *Eunuchs in Antiquity and Beyond* (London: Classical Press of Wales and Duckworth, 2002).

Tougher, Shaun, *The Eunuch in Byzantine History and Society* (London: Routledge, 2008).

Tracy, Larissa (ed.), *Castration and Culture in the Middle Ages* (Cambridge, UK: D.S. Brewer, 2013).

Türkmenoglu, Ali, *Das Strafrecht des klassischen islamischen Rechts: mit einem Vergleich zwischen der islamitischen und der modernen deutschen Strafrechslehre* (Frankfurt am Main: Peter Lang, 2013).

Turner, Bryan S., *The Body and Society*, 3rd edn. (Los Angeles: Sage, 2008).

Upson-Saia, Kristi, 'Resurrecting Deformity: Augustine on Wounded and Sacred Bodies in the Heavenly Realm', in *Disability in Judaism, Christianity, and Islam: Sacred Texts, Historical Traditions, and Social Analysis*, ed. Daria Schumm and Michael Stoltzfus (New York: Palgrave Macmillan, 2001), 93-122.

Van Yelyr, R.G., *The Whip and the Rod* (London: G. Swan, 1941).

Veldhuizen, Martine, 'De ongetemde tong. Opvattingen over zondige, onvertogen en misdadige woorden in het Middelnederlands (1300-1550)' (unpublished PhD dissertation, Utrecht University, 2013).

VerSteeg, Russ, *Law in Ancient Egypt* (Durham, NC: Carolina Academic Press, 2002).

Vogüé, Adalbert de, *Histoire littéraire du mouvement monastique dans l'Antiquité*, vol. 1 (Paris: Du Cerf, 1991).

Weisser, Michael R., *Crime and Punishment in Early Modern Europe* (Hassocks, UK: The Harvester Press, 1979).

Westbrook, Raymond (ed.), *A History of Ancient Near Eastern Law*, 2 vols. [successively numbered] (Leiden: Brill, 2003).

Wheatley, Edward, *Stumbling Blocks Before the Blind: Medieval Constructs of a Disability* (Ann Arbor: University of Michigan Press, 2010).

Whitman, James Q., *Harsh Justice: Criminal Punishment and the Widening Divide between America and Europe* (New York: Oxford University Press, 2004).

Yawn, Lila, 'The Bright Side of the Knife: Dismemberment in Medieval Europe and the Modern Imagination', in *Wounds in the Middle Ages*, ed. Anne Kirkham and Cordelia Warr (Farnham, UK: Ashgate, 2014), 215-246.

Websites

http://chartsbin.com/view/eqq

http://edition.cnn.com/2014/01/16/justice/ohio-dennis-mcguire-execution

http://endcorporalpunishment.org/pages/frame.html

http://tarlton.law.utexas.edu/exhibits/ww_justice/ruiz_v_estelle.html

http://www.afp.com/en/node/1130891

http://www.amnesty.org.uk/news_details.asp?NewsID=20725

http://www.corpun.com/rules.htm

http://www.corpun.com/vids.htm

http://www.deathpenaltyinfo.org/methods-execution

http://www.falk-bretschneider.eu/biblio/biblio-index.htm

http://www.gpo.gov/fdsys/pkg/CHRG-111hhrg55850/html/CHRG-111hhrg55850.htm

http://www.jewishencyclopedia.com/articles/4672-corporal-punishment

http://www.jewishvirtuallibrary.org/jsource/judaica/ejud_0002_0007_0_06574.html

http://www.liveleak.com/view?i=3c9_1304013159

http://www.nytimes.com/2014/07/24/us/arizona-takes-nearly-2-hours-to-execute-inmate.html?hp&action=click&pgtype=Homepage&version=HpSum&module=first-column-region&region=top-news&WT.nav=top-news

Index